My Son, Hear My Words

Notes on Proverbs

Andy Sochor

My Son, Hear My Words: Notes on Proverbs
Copyright © 2013 by Andy Sochor

All Rights Reserved. No portion of this book may be reproduced in any form without the written permission of the publisher, except in the case of brief excerpts to be used in a review.

Published by:
Gospel Armory Publishing
Bowling Green, Kentucky
www.GospelArmory.com

Unless otherwise indicated, Scripture quotations taken from the New American Standard Bible®, Copyright © 1960, 1962, 1963, 1968, 1971, 1972, 1973, 1975, 1977, 1995 by The Lockman Foundation. Used by permission.

Printed in the United States of America

ISBN: 978-0-9831046-8-1

Preface

The book of Proverbs is filled with practical wisdom that can be used in everyday life. It shows us the wisdom that comes from above and calls us to pursue that instead of the wisdom of the world.

The purpose of the book of Proverbs can be found in the opening verses:

> *"The proverbs of Solomon the son of David, king of Israel: to know wisdom and instruction, to discern the sayings of understanding, to receive instruction in wise behavior, righteousness, justice and equity; to give prudence to the naive, to the youth knowledge and discretion, a wise man will hear and increase in learning, and a man of understanding will acquire wise counsel, to understand a proverb and a figure, the words of the wise and their riddles"* (1:1-6).

These verses mention five things this study is designed to do and will help us do:

1. *To know* **wisdom and instruction** – The book of Proverbs is about wisdom. It teaches us how to acquire wisdom and provides instructions showing us how to act with wisdom.

2. *To discern* **the sayings of understanding** – As we study the book of Proverbs, we will see that it is written in such a way that we can comprehend it. Its simplicity allows us to more easily understand it and then apply what we learn.
3. *To receive* **instruction in wise behavior, righteousness, justice, and equity** – In Proverbs we receive instruction showing us how to walk in wisdom, how to be righteous, and how to be just in our dealings with others and treat everyone fairly.
4. *To give* **prudence to the naive, to the youth knowledge and discretion** – Those who lack wisdom are able to gain it from a study of Proverbs. It is designed for those who are young and inexperienced so that they may learn from one who already possesses the wisdom they might hope to attain.
5. *To grow* **as a child of God** – Though the wise man says this book is directed especially toward *"the youth,"* (1:4), it is not exclusively for them. All men, from every stage of life, can learn and grow from studying the counsel contained in the book of Proverbs. We are told what *will* happen when one approaches the book properly. First, he will *hear* and be receptive to the words of wisdom. Second, after *hearing*, he will *increase in learning*. Finally, after *learning* what he is taught, he will *acquire* wisdom.

As we begin a study of the book of Proverbs and strive to *"understand a proverb and a figure, the words of the wise and their riddles"* (1:6), I encourage you to remember what the wise man says: *"A wise man will hear and increase in learning, and a man of understanding will acquire wise counsel"* (1:5).

The book of Proverbs reveals the wisdom that comes from above. If you desire this wisdom, then you will eagerly read and study the words that have been recorded. The simplicity of the Proverbs makes it so that your eager reading and studying (*hearing*) will result in *learning*. The truths discussed in this book are not unattainable for the common man, only to be comprehended by the elite. These truths are for *everyone*. As you learn the words of wisdom and put them into practice, you will gain wisdom yourself – not *worldly* wisdom, but wisdom that comes from above.

So I invite you to follow along in this study. May we all grow in wisdom as we study the book of Proverbs.

Table of Contents

Preface	iii
Introduction to the Book of Proverbs	1
The Appeal of Wisdom	11
The Appreciation of Wisdom	27
The Appreciation of Wisdom: Contrast Between the Righteous and the Wicked	47
The Acquisition of Wisdom	59
The Application of Wisdom	87
The Application of Wisdom: Character	91
The Application of Wisdom: Speech	103
The Application of Wisdom: Work	123
The Application of Wisdom: Stewardship	135
The Application of Wisdom: Justice	153
The Application of Wisdom: Suffering	159

The Application of Wisdom: Alcohol	163
The Application of Wisdom: Plans for the Future	169
The Application of Wisdom: Women	173
The Application of Wisdom: Family	201
The Application of Wisdom: Friendship	211
The Application of Wisdom: Neighbors	223
The Application of Wisdom: Government	237
The Application of Wisdom: God	251
Conclusion	267
Works Referenced	271
Scripture Index	273
Additional Resources	281

Introduction to the Book of Proverbs

Many books have been written in which the author claims to be imparting some wisdom to his readers. What makes the book of Proverbs different is the author and the source of his wisdom.

The Author of Proverbs

The last two chapters of Proverbs are attributed to *"Agur the son of Jakeh, the oracle"* (30:1) and *"King Lemuel, the oracle which his mother taught him"* (31:1). The identities of these individuals are uncertain. However, the bulk of Proverbs can be attributed to *"Solomon, the son of David, king of Israel"* (1:1). Some of these *"proverbs of Solomon"* were *"transcribed"* by *"the men of Hezekiah, king of Judah"* (25:1).

It is important that we understand how Solomon acquired his wisdom. We find the answer to this shortly after Solomon established his rule as king over Israel.

> *"In Gibeon the Lord appeared to Solomon in a dream at night; and **God said, 'Ask what you wish Me to give you.'** Then Solomon said, 'You have shown great lovingkindness to Your servant David my father, according as he walked before You in truth and righteousness and uprightness of heart toward You; and You have reserved for him this great*

lovingkindness, that You have given him a son to sit on his throne, as it is this day. Now, O Lord my God, You have made Your servant king in place of my father David, yet I am but a little child; I do not know how to go out or come in. Your servant is in the midst of Your people which You have chosen, a great people who are too many to be numbered or counted. **So give Your servant an understanding heart to judge Your people to discern between good and evil.** *For who is able to judge this great people of Yours?'*

"It was pleasing in the sight of the Lord that Solomon had asked this thing. God said to him, 'Because you have asked this thing and have not asked for yourself long life, nor have asked riches for yourself, nor have you asked for the life of your enemies, but have asked for yourself discernment to understand justice, behold, I have done according to your words. **Behold, I have given you a wise and discerning heart, so that there has been no one like you before you, nor shall one like you arise after you**'" (1 Kings 3:5-12).

It is certainly true that no one could equal Solomon in terms of wisdom. When the queen of Sheba heard of Solomon's wisdom and traveled to visit him in order to see for herself if the reports were true, she discovered that they were absolutely true.

"Then she said to the king, 'It was a true report which I heard in my own land about your words and your wisdom. Nevertheless I did not believe the

> *reports, until I came and my eyes had seen it. And behold, the half was not told me. You exceed in wisdom and prosperity the report which I heard'"* (1 Kings 10:6-7).

God promised to give Solomon wisdom. When He did, the evidence of this wisdom was so overwhelming that a ruler from another land confirmed that Solomon's wisdom was far greater than anything she had been told about him.

Solomon's wisdom was miraculously granted to Him by God. This is not going to happen to us today. It will take more time and effort on our part, but we can certainly gain wisdom. Notice what James wrote:

> *"But if any of you lacks wisdom, let him ask of God, who gives to all generously and without reproach, and it will be given to him. But he must ask in faith without any doubting, for the one who doubts is like the surf of the sea, driven and tossed by the wind"* (James 1:5-6).

After Solomon was given wisdom directly from God, he wrote down his wise teachings of the book of Proverbs. Why? If God would miraculously grant everyone wisdom who desired it, this written volume would be superfluous. He wrote these things down so that others could read them and receive instruction in the ways of wisdom.

It is important to note that even though Solomon was given wisdom directly and miraculously from God, he still possessed the characteristics necessary to receive wisdom – characteristics we must have if we wish to gain wisdom:

1. **Solomon recognized God as the source of all blessings.** When God asked Solomon to ask Him for what he wished, the king's first response was to acknowledge God's great blessings up to that point. *"You have shown great lovingkindness to Your servant David my father"* (1 Kings 3:6). If we hope to gain the wisdom that comes from above, we must also recognize what James wrote: *"Every good thing given and every perfect gift is from above, coming down from the Father of lights"* (James 1:17).
2. **Solomon was humble.** Though he had become king, Solomon recognized that he was *"but a little child"* who did not *"know how to go out or come in"* (1 Kings 3:7). We, too, must possess humility if we are to gain wisdom. We *"acquire wisdom"* by heeding the *"words"* of those who are teaching us of the wisdom that comes from above (4:5). James said that *"in humility,"* we are to *"receive the word implanted"* (James 1:21).
3. **Solomon appreciated his responsibility.** Solomon recognized that he was ruling over *"a great people"* that had been *"chosen"* by God (1 Kings 3:8). The enormity of his responsibility, coupled with his humility noted in the previous point, caused him to realize that he needed wisdom and to desire it.
4. **Solomon was selfless, putting others first.** Solomon could have asked God for long life, riches, or the life of his enemies (1 Kings 3:11); but he did not. Instead of asking for something that would be of primary benefit to himself, he asked for something that would benefit others –

"an understanding heart to judge [the] people" (1 Kings 3:9). The wisdom of the world focuses on self-promotion and self-preservation. The wisdom that comes from above causes us to seek the good of others as we are told to love our neighbors as ourselves (Leviticus 19:18; Matthew 22:39).

If we possess these characteristics that Solomon demonstrated when he was granted wisdom by God, we will also gain wisdom as we follow the source of wisdom.

However, there is another important lesson to be learned from Solomon. We can learn from his example that the pursuit and possession of wisdom alone is not enough.

"Now King Solomon loved many foreign women along with the daughter of Pharaoh: Moabite, Ammonite, Edomite, Sidonian, and Hittite women, from the nations concerning which the Lord had said to the sons of Israel, 'You shall not associate with them, nor shall they associate with you, for they will surely turn your heart away after other gods.' Solomon held fast to these in love. He had seven hundred wives, princesses, and three hundred concubines, and his wives turned his heart away.

"For when Solomon was old, his wives turned his heart away after other gods; and his heart was not wholly devoted to the Lord his God, as the heart of David his father had been. For Solomon went after Ashtoreth the goddess of the Sidonians and after Milcom the detestable idol of the Ammonites.

> *Solomon did what was evil in the sight of the Lord, and did not follow the Lord fully, as David his father had done. Then Solomon built a high place for Chemosh the detestable idol of Moab, on the mountain which is east of Jerusalem, and for Molech the detestable idol of the sons of Ammon. Thus also he did for all his foreign wives, who burned incense and sacrificed to their gods"* (1 Kings 11:1-8).

Solomon knew better. He possessed wisdom in the ways of God. Yet he did not use this wisdom. Instead, he ignored the will of God and followed the godless influence of those who were close to him. It is not enough to *pursue* wisdom, or even to *possess* wisdom; we must *use* the wisdom we have.

The Subject Matter of Proverbs

Under the broad category of *wisdom*, the book of Proverbs discusses many different subjects. It deals with the pursuit of wisdom itself. It includes practical instruction for living. It discusses matters relating to personal growth, our dealings with others, proper conduct in society, and appropriate service to God. These subjects are scattered throughout the book. This material arranges the various proverbs according to topic in order to help us in our study of the book.

The book of Proverbs breaks down into four basic areas:

1. **The *appeal* of wisdom** – This is done in two ways. First, the wise man *appeals* to his son to heed his words of wisdom: *"Hear, my son, your father's instruction and do not forsake your mother's teaching"* (1:8). Second, wisdom is personified

and makes an *appeal* for man to follow after her: *"Wisdom shouts in the street, she lifts her voice in the square"* (1:20).

2. **The *appreciation* of wisdom** – Once we recognize the *appeal* of wisdom, this second part explains why we are to listen by telling us to *appreciate* wisdom. This is done by pointing out the benefits and blessings that come when we follow after wisdom: *"Riches and honor are with me* [wisdom, see 8:12], *enduring wealth and righteousness. My fruit is better than gold, even pure gold, and my yield better than choicest silver"* (8:18-19).

3. **The *acquisition* of wisdom** – After hearing the *appeal* of wisdom and learning why we should *appreciate* wisdom, we will see instructions and encouragement that will lead us to *acquire* wisdom: *"Acquire wisdom! Acquire understanding! Do not forget nor turn away from the words of my mouth"* (4:5). *"The beginning of wisdom is: Acquire wisdom; and with all your acquiring, get understanding"* (4:7).

4. **The *application* of wisdom** – Simply acquiring wisdom is not the goal. Wisdom must be put into practice. Solomon says, *"Doing wickedness is like a sport to a fool, and so is wisdom to a man of understanding"* (10:23). A fool is not just one who lacks wisdom. A fool also *practices* wickedness. In the same way, one who has *understanding* will *apply* his wisdom and put it into practice.

How to Interpret Proverbs

When we study the book of Proverbs, we need to understand that it contains general statements about life. It is not talking about absolute rewards, punishments, or consequences that exist in this life that come as a result of either *wise* living or *foolish* living. Notice just a couple of examples:

"*Train up a child in the way he should go, even when he is old he will not depart from it*" (22:6). This statement is *generally* true. However, we all know godly parents who did all they could in raising their children the right way, only to have their children forsake the Lord after they had grown. Every person has free will. Sadly, some choose to forsake the good instruction they received from godly parents and follow a path which they should not go.

"*He who tills his land will have plenty of food, but he who follows empty pursuits will have poverty in plenty*" (28:19). Again, this is a statement that is *generally* true. However, there are occasionally times of drought, sickness, injury, or other hardships that might prevent the diligent worker from enjoying the fruit of his labor.

As they pertain to this life, the rewards, punishments, and consequences mentioned in Proverbs are *generally* true. However, if we follow the wisdom that comes from above, the reward we have to look forward to later is *absolutely* true. Solomon says, "*The righteous has a refuge when he dies*" (14:32), and wisdom "*is a tree of life to those who take hold of her*" (3:18).

In interpreting Proverbs, it is also important to remember what Solomon says near the beginning of the book:

> *"The fear of the Lord is the beginning of knowledge;*
> *fools despise wisdom and instruction"* (1:7).

If we pursue divine wisdom in the fear of the Lord – respecting Him enough to trust Him and follow His instructions – we will certainly profit from a study of the book of Proverbs.

The Appeal of Wisdom

The invitation to take hold of the wisdom that comes from above is universal. It is expressed in two ways in the book of Proverbs. First, we read of a father inviting his son to take heed to his words: *"My son, give attention to my words; incline your ear to my sayings"* (4:20). Second, we read of wisdom personified extending the invitation for all to come, learn, and become wise: *"Does not wisdom call, and understanding lift up her voice? [...] 'To you, O men, I call, and my voice is to the sons of men. O naive ones, understand prudence; and, O fools, understand wisdom. Listen, for I will speak noble things..."* (8:1, 4-6).

The Father's Appeal

> *"My son, do not forget my teaching, but let your heart keep my commandments; for length of days and years of life and peace they will add to you. Do not let kindness and truth leave you; bind them around your neck, write them on the tablet of your heart. So you will find favor and good repute in the sight of God and man"* (3:1-4).

An earlier statement in the book is similar to this: *"Hear, my son, your father's instruction and do not forsake your mother's teaching"* (1:8). The earlier passage introduces the father's specific instruction about friendships and evil influences that will be considered later in our study. The above passage (3:1-4) is more general; so for our purposes we will begin with it.

***"My son, do not forget my teaching, but let your heart keep my commandments"* (3:1).** The father's instruction that his son *"not forget"* his teaching implies that his son had already been taught. The father is simply *reminding* his son of what he has instructed previously. The father's invitation then is for the son to *hear* and *accept* his teaching, *retain* his teaching (*"not forget"*), and *apply* his teaching (*"keep my commandments"*).

***"For length of days and years of life and peace they will add to you"* (3:2).** Why should the son listen to his father's instruction? He should listen, not just because of the authority his father has over him, but because he will benefit from heeding his father's command. The children of Israel were told, *"Honor your father and your mother, as the Lord your God has commanded you, that your days may be prolonged and that it may go well with you on the land which the Lord your God gives you"* (Deuteronomy 5:16). Similarly, the wise man tells his son that by *accepting, retaining,* and *applying* his teaching, he will be blessed for many years. This, of course, is *generally*, not *absolutely*, true.

***"Do not let kindness and truth leave you; bind them around your neck, write them on the tablet of your heart"* (3:3).** The father again tells his son to *retain* his instructions. In this verse, he tells him to do this in two ways. To *"bind them around your neck"* suggests an outward manifestation of the son's retention of his father's teaching (actions, words). To *"write them on the tablet of your heart"* describes how his father's instructions were to govern his inward being (thoughts, motives). The point is that the wisdom the father imparts to his son, and the wisdom found throughout the book of Proverbs, is for the *whole* man (actions, words, thoughts, and motives).

***"So you will find favor and good repute in the sight of God and man"* (3:4).** The father mentions a twofold benefit of following his words of wisdom. First, his son would *"find favor...in the sight of God."* As previously noted, a healthy *"fear of the Lord is the beginning of knowledge"* (1:7) and *"wisdom"* (9:10). One must follow after divine wisdom to be pleasing to God. Second, his son would be of *"good repute in the sight of...man."* The application of the wisdom imparted by this father and discussed throughout the book of Proverbs is practical and can be easily seen and will be respected by others.

Wisdom's Appeal

> *"Wisdom shouts in the street, she lifts her voice in the square; at the head of the noisy streets she cries out; at the entrance of the gates in the city she utters her sayings: 'How long, O naive ones, will you love being simple-minded? And scoffers delight themselves in scoffing and fools hate knowledge? Turn to my reproof, behold, I will pour out my spirit on you; I will make my words known to you. Because I called and you refused, I stretched out my hand and no one paid attention; and you neglected all my counsel and did not want my reproof; I will also laugh at your calamity; I will mock when your dread comes, when your dread comes like a storm and your calamity comes like a whirlwind, when distress and anguish come upon you. Then they will*

call on me, but I will not answer; they will seek me diligently but they will not find me, because they hated knowledge and did not choose the fear of the Lord. They would not accept my counsel, they spurned all my reproof. So they shall eat of the fruit of their own way and be satiated with their own devices. For the waywardness of the naive will kill them, and the complacency of fools will destroy them. But he who listens to me shall live securely and will be at ease from the dread of evil" (1:20-33).

This is the first of three passages we will be considering in which the wise man personifies wisdom and describes her *appealing* to man to take heed to her.

"Wisdom shouts in the street, she lifts her voice in the square; at the head of the noisy streets she cries out; at the entrance of the gates in the city she utters her sayings" (1:20-21). The fact that Wisdom is being described as shouting and crying out in the *street*, in the *square*, at the head of the *noisy streets*, and at the *entry gates* to the city is meant to show us that the call of Wisdom is made *publicly* and *openly* to all. Yet there is no mention of a crowd gathering around, eager to learn from the one proclaiming wisdom; only an inattentive refusal to receive wisdom (1:24-25). The lesson is that though Wisdom calls to all, not all will obtain wisdom. Therefore, if one does not grow in wisdom, it is because he has *rejected* wisdom, not because wisdom was inaccessible to him. We have already noticed the father imparting wisdom to his son (3:1-4). What if there is no father to impart wisdom? What if the father is unwilling or unable to teach his son? Though the son in such situations would certainly be at a disadvantage, there is still wisdom to be gained as it is calling out to all, openly and freely.

"'How long, O naive ones, will you love being simple-minded? And scoffers delight themselves in scoffing and fools hate knowledge?'" (1:22). Incredibly, there are many people who prefer life without wisdom – at least the *divine* wisdom that is being offered to them here. They *"love being simple-minded"* and *"hate knowledge."* We often hear the phrase, "ignorance is bliss." To those who are willingly foolish and naive, this is their motto. They know just enough about the wisdom that invites them that they have convinced themselves that they want no part of it. Instead they *"delight themselves in scoffing,"* preferring to ridicule and mock rather than learn and grow. But why would so many people prefer simple-mindedness and foolishness over the wisdom that comes from above? Solomon gives an answer to this in the next verse.

"'Turn to my reproof, behold, I will pour out my spirit on you; I will make my words known to you'" (1:23). For one to abandon his foolishness in order to take hold of wisdom, he must first receive *reproof*. He must be shown how he is in error so that he can make correction and follow what is right. This key component in gaining wisdom – *reproof* – is uncomfortable and undesirable to many. People do not want to have their faults pointed out to them and be told that they must now do something differently. This is why many reject divine wisdom. As we will discuss more in depth later in this study, we can infer from this passage that we must be willing to listen to reproof, admit wrong, and make corrections in our lives. If we are willing to do these things, Wisdom says she *will* pour out her spirit on us and make her words known to us. If we apply ourselves to wisdom with the proper attitude, we *will* be able to acquire it.

"'Because I called and you refused, I stretched out my hand and no one paid attention; and you neglected all my counsel and did not want my reproof'" (1:24-25). God never forces anyone to hear, learn, obey, or grow. We must *choose* to do those things. In the same way, the wisdom that comes down from above will not be forced upon us. Wisdom will *call*, but we can *refuse*. We are free to *choose* to pay no attention to the appeal of Wisdom. But there will be consequences, as they are mentioned in the verses that follow.

"I will also laugh at your calamity; I will mock when your dread comes, when your dread comes like a storm and your calamity comes like a whirlwind, when distress and anguish come upon you" (1:26-27). Wisdom is described as *laughing* and *mocking* when trouble comes to those who refused to listen. To us, this may seem a little harsh. But it is no more harsh than the fool's rejection of the appeal that was made to him by Wisdom. Also, it is important to note that this *calamity* is spoken of as a certainty. The text does not say Wisdom will mock *if* dread and distress come; it says that Wisdom will mock *when* dread and distress come. There are negative consequences that come as a result of one rejecting Wisdom. The timing and severity of these consequences will vary, but the fact that they *will* come is a certainty.

"Then they will call on me, but I will not answer; they will seek me diligently but they will not find me, because they hated knowledge and did not choose the fear of the Lord. They would not accept my counsel, they spurned all my reproof" (1:28-30). We might wonder: if Wisdom was previously crying out, why will she refuse to answer when these pepole start calling on her and diligently seeking her? The reason is because *"they hated knowledge and did not choose the fear of the Lord."* They rejected the *counsel* and *reproof* of wisdom. We might then wonder: does God not allow one who had previously rejected Him and His wisdom to repent? Of course He does (cf. Ezekiel 18:32; 2 Peter 3:9). But even if one repents, he will still have to face the negative consequences of the choices he made prior to his repentance. Therefore, since these individuals rejected the wisdom that could have prevented their calamity, even a penitent heart would not deliver them from the *physical consequences* of their prior decisions. Acquiring wisdom is a process. If we forsake the appeal of Wisdom until we need wisdom, it will be too late. We must grow in wisdom *now* in order to prepare for the future.

"So they shall eat of the fruit of their own way and be satiated with their own devices. For the waywardness of the naive will kill them, and the complacency of fools will destroy them" (1:31-32). When calamity comes, those who rejected Wisdom will have to suffer the consequences of their rejection. The seed that they sowed in foolishness will bear fruit. Those who rejected Wisdom will eat of this fruit (experience the negative consequences of their choices) and be *satiated*. This means they would be filled to the point of disgust, just as when one becomes sick from eating too much of an unhealthy food. The *"waywardness of the naive"* brings about death, reminding us again that ignorance is *not* bliss. The *complacency*, or *prosperity* (KJV), of fools brings destruction. As long as they are content in their foolishness and naivete, they will develop no desire to seek after wisdom.

***"But he who listens to me shall live securely and will be at ease from the dread of evil'"* (1:33).** Just as there are negative consequences for rejecting Wisdom, there is also a reward for accepting Wisdom. More of the benefits of wisdom will be discussed later in the study. But here Solomon tells us that those who listen to the words of Wisdom will enjoy *security* and *peace* from the threat of calamity that would be against those who rejected Wisdom.

* * *

> *"Does not wisdom call, and understanding lift up her voice? On top of the heights beside the way, where the paths meet, she takes her stand; beside the gates, at the opening to the city, at the entrance of the doors, she cries out: 'To you, O men, I call, and my voice is to the sons of men. O naive ones, understand prudence; and, O fools, understand wisdom. Listen, for I will speak noble things; and the opening of my lips will reveal right things. For my mouth will utter truth; and wickedness is an abomination to my lips. All the utterances of my mouth are in righteousness; there is nothing crooked or perverted in them. They are all straightforward to him who understands, and right to those who find knowledge. Take my instruction and not silver, and knowledge rather than choicest gold. For wisdom is better than jewels; and all desirable things cannot compare with her"* (8:1-11).

This second passage describing Wisdom's appeal to man contains an invitation that explains, in general terms, the teachings of Wisdom. It also introduces the value of wisdom.

"Does not wisdom call, and understanding lift up her voice? On top of the heights beside the way, where the paths meet, she takes her stand; beside the gates, at the opening to the city, at the entrance of the doors, she cries out" **(8:1-3).** The question in the first verse is rhetorical. Of course Wisdom calls and lifts her voice. As we have already noticed, this call is made *publicly*, indicating that it is open to all (cf. 1:20-21).

"'To you, O men, I call, and my voice is to the sons of men. O naive ones, understand prudence; and, O fools, understand wisdom'" **(8:4-5).** This further emphasizes the need for all to take heed unto the call of Wisdom. The wisdom that comes from above is intended for *"the sons of men."* God expects people to gain wisdom and has made it so that all are able to do so. It is designed to give prudence and wisdom to those who are naive and foolish. Calling these ones *naive* and *foolish* is not meant to be an insult. Certainly all people, at some point in their lives, have a time when they are naive and foolish simply because they have not yet learned what they need to know. The point is that we should not *remain* in a state of naivete and foolishness.

"Listen, for I will speak noble things; and the opening of my lips will reveal right things. For my mouth will utter truth; and wickedness is an abomination to my lips. All the utterances of my mouth are in righteousness; there is nothing crooked or perverted in them" **(8:6-8).** The wisdom that comes from above is different from the wisdom of the world (cf. 1 Corinthians 1:20-21). Because man is fallible, the wisdom of the world is fallible. Paul would later write, *"For the wisdom of this world is foolishness before God"* (1 Corinthians 3:19). In contrast, because God is *infallible*, the wisdom that comes from above is *perfect*. As Wisdom describes her teaching, we see a

perfect message that has come from an *infallible* being. Wisdom speaks of things which are *noble* and *right* (3:6). The word translated *noble* or *excellent* (KJV) is used elsewhere to describe those in positions of civil or military power. It indicates that the words of Wisdom are *superior* over the worldly wisdom that is contrary to it. The lips of Wisdom speak *truth* and not *wickedness* (3:7). The teachings of Wisdom are wholly *righteous*, containing no hint of any error or foolishness (3:8).

"They are all straightforward to him who understands, and right to those who find knowledge" (8:9). The previous verses describe the sayings of Wisdom as being wholly noble, right, true, and righteous. However, not everyone is going to accept the wisdom that comes from above as being these things. Many follow the wisdom of the world, believing it is more noble, right, true, and righteous than the wisdom that comes from above. Why do some reject godly wisdom for worldly wisdom? It is because they do not understand or have knowledge. One who truly understands and appreciates the difference between the two types of wisdom will always choose to follow after the wisdom that comes from above. Those who follow the wisdom of the world either do not *know* the wisdom that comes from God, or they have not put forth enough of an effort to *understand* it.

"Take my instruction and not silver, and knowledge rather than choicest gold. For wisdom is better than jewels; and all desirable things cannot compare with her" (8:10-11). We will discuss more later in the study about the value of wisdom. The idea is introduced to us here. Those things which man values in this life – silver, gold, jewels, and any other desirable possession – cannot compare with the wisdom that comes from above. Therefore, Wisdom calls us to listen to her *instruction* and gain the *knowledge* that will lead one to acquire wisdom.

* * *

> *"Wisdom has built her house, she has hewn out her seven pillars; she has prepared her food, she has mixed her wine; she has also set her table; she has sent out her maidens, she calls from the tops of the heights of the city: 'Whoever is naive, let him turn in here!' To him who lacks understanding she says, 'Come, eat of my food and drink of the wine I have mixed. Forsake your folly and live, and proceed in the way of understanding'"* (9:1-6).

The final passage we will notice that describes Wisdom's appeal presents a picture of wisdom making preparations to host a feast and inviting others to attend.

"Wisdom has built her house, she has hewn out her seven pillars; she has prepared her food, she has mixed her wine; she has also set her table; she has sent out her maidens, she calls from the tops of the heights of the city" (9:1-3). The fact that Wisdom has built a house, as opposed to pitching a tent, indicates that it is firmly established. The *seven* pillars indicate *completeness*, that it is lacking in nothing. Preparations are made for this feast, and the invitations are sent. The call for men to attend the feast is done *"from the tops of the heights of the city,"* again, indicates a *public* invitation that is made to *all* (cf. 1:20-21; 8:2-3).

"'Whoever is naive, let him turn in here!' To him who lacks understanding she says, 'Come, eat of my food and drink of

***the wine I have mixed. Forsake your folly and live, and proceed in the way of understanding'"* (9:4-6).** The invitation is directed to those who are *naive* and who *lack understanding*. Of course, all who lack wisdom from above need to answer this call. But one must be *humble* enough to recognize the fact that he is *naive* and lacking in understanding. Those who are rebellious or arrogant, though they are in need of godly wisdom, will not answer the call because they do not believe that they need it. We must be able to acknowledge our shortcomings and humbly seek after this wisdom. After one humbly receives wise instruction, he must repent (*forsake his folly*) and do the will of God (*proceed in the way of understanding*). It will not do any good for one to *learn* of the right way, then fail to give up his wickedness and follow after what is right. *Acquiring* wisdom must necessarily result in one *applying* wisdom. Most of the book of Proverbs is devoted to this *application* of wisdom.

The Timeless Nature of Wisdom

After considering the *appeal* of wisdom – both from a father and from Wisdom itself – it is important to consider whether or not this same wisdom is good for us today. The wisdom we are considering in the book of Proverbs is not *worldly* wisdom but wisdom that comes from above. As Solomon explains in the following passage, godly wisdom will *never* become obsolete or irrelevant. For this reason, Wisdom also appeals to us.

> "The Lord possessed me at the beginning of His way, before His works of old. From everlasting I was established, from the beginning, from the earliest times of the earth. When there were no depths I was

> *brought forth, when there were no springs abounding with water. Before the mountains were settled, before the hills I was brought forth; while He had not yet made the earth and the fields, nor the first dust of the world. When He established the heavens, I was there, when He inscribed a circle on the face of the deep, when He made firm the skies above, when the springs of the deep became fixed, when He set for the sea its boundary so that the water would not transgress His command, when He marked out the foundations of the earth; then I was beside Him, as a master workman; and I was daily His delight, rejoicing always before Him, rejoicing in the world, His earth, and having my delight in the sons of men.*
>
> *"Now therefore, O sons, listen to me, for blessed are they who keep my ways. Heed instruction and be wise, and do not neglect it. Blessed is the man who listens to me, watching daily at my gates, waiting at my doorposts. For he who finds me finds life and obtains favor from the Lord. But he who sins against me injures himself; all those who hate me love death"* (8:22-36).

Wisdom is timeless. It existed before, during, and after the Creation. The wise man explains here why this is important.

"The Lord possessed me at the beginning of His way, before His works of old" (8:22). Wisdom is speaking here, reminding us that the wisdom we are considering is not the worldly wisdom of man. Therefore, the wisdom that we are to pursue is older than the world itself. It belongs to God, not to man; so we must look to God and to what He has revealed in order to acquire this wisdom.

"From everlasting I was established, from the beginning, from the earliest times of the earth" **(8:23).** There are three periods of time mentioned in this verse. First, there is the time *before* Creation (*"from everlasting"*). Second, there is the time *of* the Creation (*"from the beginning"*). Finally, there is the time in which man has inhabited the earth (*"from the earliest times of the earth"*) – which has been since the sixth day at the end of the Creation week, right before God *"completed His work"* and *"rested on the seventh day"* (Genesis 1:26-2:2). This means that divine wisdom predates any human society or culture. Man often takes pride in how the culture in which he is a part has grown and progressed throughout generations, gaining collective wisdom along the way. Much of this wisdom, though, is *worldly* wisdom. *Godly* wisdom came before all of this, and so it is independent of human reasoning. Therefore, what may be considered "common sense" or some enlightened realization by a particular society – even our modern society – is not necessarily true or wise. True wisdom existed since before Creation, during the Creation, and from the beginning of man. In the following verses, Solomon expands on these time periods.

"Before the mountains…before the hills…while He had not yet made the earth…nor the first dust of the world" **(8:24-25).** Before *"the beginning"* in which *"God created the heavens and the earth"* (Genesis 1:1), God *"brought forth"* wisdom. This Wisdom that appeals to us to *"listen"* (8:32) is older than time. Therefore, we should not expect it to change with time.

"When He established the heavens...when He inscribed a circle on the face of the deep, when He made firm the skies...when the springs of the deep became fixed, when He set for the sea its boundary...when He marked out the foundations of the earth" **(8:27-29).** Wisdom existed with God prior to Creation, then was used by God in creating the heavens and the earth. These verses describe that work of Creation. All that was created and continues to be sustained by His providence is a testament to the wisdom of God.

"Then I was beside Him, as a master workman; and I was daily His delight, rejoicing always before Him, rejoicing in the world, His earth, and having my delight in the sons of men" **(8:30-31).** Wisdom is closely connected to God's work in Creation, being *"beside Him,"* with Him *"daily,"* and *"always before Him."* This suggests that for us to possess true wisdom, we must acknowledge God as the Creator. To reject Him as the Creator is to reject the wisdom that existed *"beside Him, as a master workman."* At the end, we learn that Wisdom's *"delight [is] with the sons of men"* (KJV). This wisdom exists for our benefit. The creation and subsequent providence, which are grounded in wisdom, are for our good. The divine message of wisdom that is revealed from above is for our good as well. As we continue this study, we will see many ways in which wisdom benefits those who follow after it.

"Now therefore, O sons, listen to me, for blessed are they who keep my ways. Heed instruction and be wise, and do not neglect it" **(8:32-33).** Similar to what we have already noticed, Wisdom invites all to *listen, heed,* and become wise. Following this type of instruction must invariably lead to obedience. If we keep the ways of wisdom, we will be blessed. Conversely, if we neglect the ways of wisdom, then not only can we not

expect the blessings, but we can expect negative consequences for this neglect. Not only must we gain wisdom, but we must regularly be reminded of the things which we have been taught so that, as the Hebrew writer stated, *"we do not drift away from it"* (Hebrews 2:1).

***"Blessed is the man who listens to me, watching daily at my gates, waiting at my doorposts. For he who finds me finds life and obtains favor from the Lord"* (8:34-35).** To be blessed we must *listen* to the words of Wisdom. Furthermore, we must exhibit patience and a willingness to wait daily upon Wisdom's instruction. Wisdom will never be obtained overnight. Therefore, we must diligently study so that we can have her teachings firmly planted in our minds. If we do this and follow after this wisdom, then we will find life and the Lord's favor.

***"But he who sins against me injures himself; all those who hate me love death"* (8:36).** While there are certainly benefits to following Wisdom, there are also negative consequences for rejecting her. When we forsake the wisdom that comes from above, we bring harm to ourselves and demonstrate that we *"love death."*

The next section of our study will focus on the good that is gained and the evil that is avoided by following Wisdom so that we might develop a proper *appreciation* of wisdom.

The Appreciation of Wisdom

We have already considered passages discussing the *appeal* of wisdom, calling us to gain the instruction and insight necessary to acquire wisdom. But why should we answer this call? There are many invitations that may be offered that are disregarded by those who are invited. Why should we listen to the *appeal of wisdom?* It is because of the great value of wisdom, the rewards that come from following wisdom, and the perils that we face when we reject wisdom.

All of these are pointed out to us in the book of Proverbs. When God offers His wisdom which was with Him from the beginning (8:22), He does not expect us to accept it without explaining *why* we should accept it. So let us consider the reasons why we should *appreciate* wisdom so we will heed the *appeal* of wisdom.

The Value of Wisdom

The first reason why we should *appreciate* wisdom is the inherent *value* of wisdom. But before we can consider the value of wisdom, we must begin with the starting point for pursuing wisdom – truth.

> "Buy truth, and do not sell it, get wisdom and instruction and understanding" (23:23).

We must first recognize that *truth* is more valuable than anything of a material nature which we could buy or sell. We should not understand truth to mean something subjective that will change from one person, time, region, or circumstance to another. Truth is the objective standard that has been revealed from God. It is the *word* of God (cf. Psalm 119:160; John 17:17).

Truth – the revealed word of God – is the starting point that leads to wisdom. The wise man also mentions *instruction* and *understanding* as coming from truth. This tells us three things about truth (the word of God):

1. It leads to divine wisdom.
2. It is the basis for all instruction in matters that pertain to God.
3. It can be understood.

Those who look for wisdom apart from the truth of God's word are seeking the wrong kind of wisdom. Those who use a standard of authority other than the truth of God's word for their religious practices and doctrines are in error. Those who believe that the truth of God's word cannot be understood are mistaken.

Truth leads to instruction. Instruction leads to understanding. Then understanding leads to wisdom. When man produces a product to be sold, the fair market value of it is always worth *more* than the sum total of the raw materials used to make it. Truth – God's word – is valuable. The psalmist described the words of God as being *"more desirable than gold, yes, than much fine gold; sweeter also than honey and the drippings of the honeycomb"* (Psalm 19:10). How much more valuable is the wisdom that comes from a proper understanding and practice of the truth. The following passages help us to understand just how valuable the wisdom that comes from above is.

> *"Take my instruction and not silver, and knowledge rather than choicest gold. For wisdom is better than jewels; and all desirable things cannot compare with her"* (8:10-11).
>
> *"Riches and honor are with me, enduring wealth and righteousness. My fruit is better than gold, even pure gold, and my yield better than choicest silver"* (8:18-19).
>
> *"How much better it is to get wisdom than gold! And to get understanding is to be chosen above silver"* (16:16).

The first two passages have Wisdom speaking, and the third contains a statement from the wise man about wisdom. The point is clear: wisdom is far more valuable than any riches of this world. Throughout history, gold, silver, and jewels have had a great value associated with them. It is natural, then, to see these as having great worth. But no matter how valuable these are, they *"cannot compare"* with divine wisdom. If we are to gain wisdom, we must value it so highly that we will not let even gold, silver, or jewels distract us from its pursuit.

The Rewards of Wisdom

Wisdom is not valuable simply because it has been arbitrarily declared to be valuable. It is valuable because of the rewards that come for following after it.

> *"How blessed is the man who finds wisdom and the man who gains understanding. For her profit is better than the profit of silver and her gain better than fine gold. She is more precious than jewels; and nothing you desire compares with her. Long life is in her right hand; in her left hand are riches and honor. Her ways are pleasant ways and all her paths are peace. She is a tree of life to those who take hold of her, and happy are all who hold her fast. The Lord by wisdom founded the earth, by understanding He established the heavens. By His knowledge the deeps were broken up and the skies drip with dew.*
>
> *"My son, let them not vanish from your sight; keep sound wisdom and discretion, so they will be life to your soul and adornment to your neck. Then you will walk in your way securely and your foot will not stumble. When you lie down, you will not be afraid; when you lie down, your sleep will be sweet. Do not be afraid of sudden fear nor of the onslaught of the wicked when it comes; for the Lord will be your confidence and will keep your foot from being caught"* (3:13-26).

The one who finds wisdom and gains understanding is *blessed* (3:13). But how so? The wise man explains how wisdom causes one to be blessed.

"For her profit is better than the profit of silver and her gain better than fine gold. She is more precious than jewels; and nothing you desire compares with her" (3:14-15). As we have already noticed, wisdom is of far greater value than the material things of this life. Of all the things we might desire, wisdom will prove to be far more valuable as a long-term investment. Elsewhere, in contrasting the wise and the foolish, the wise man writes, *"A man will be **satisfied** with good by the fruit of his words, and the deeds of a man's hands will return to him"* (12:14). We will be *satisfied* when we apply ourselves to wisdom and reap its fruits. Therefore, we should pursue it.

"Long life is in her right hand; in her left hand are riches and honor" (3:16). One of the benefits of wisdom, generally, is *long life*, as our lives are not cut short through foolish choices and activities. When we pursue the things that lead to wisdom – righteousness, humility, and the fear of the Lord – we find *"riches, honor and life"* (22:4; cf. 21:21). A few chapters later, Wisdom says, *"For by me your days will be multiplied, and years of life will be added to you"* (9:11). Riches and honor are also often byproducts of one's *acquisition* and *application* of wisdom. Wisdom says she will *"endow those who love me with wealth, that I may fill their treasuries"* (8:21; cf. 24:3-4).

"Her ways are pleasant ways and all her paths are peace" (3:17). Following after wisdom leads to pleasant and peaceful paths for life. Later, Solomon writes, *"The path of life leads upward for the wise that he may keep away from Sheol below"* (15:24). *Upward* is in the direction of heaven and the dwelling place of God. Therefore, the wisdom that comes from above shows us the way to reach God in heaven.

"She is a tree of life to those who take hold of her, and happy are all who hold her fast" (3:18). In the beginning, man's access to the tree of life was lost because of sin (Genesis 3:22-24). Wisdom is now *"a tree of life"* for those who follow after her because, as we noticed in the previous verse, divine wisdom leads us back to heaven where the tree of life (eternal life) can be found (cf. Revelation 22:2). Elsewhere, the wise man writes, *"The fruit of the righteous is a tree of life"* (11:30). That which is produced by a life of righteousness, guided by the wisdom that comes from above, is eternal life.

"The Lord by wisdom founded the earth, by understanding He established the heavens. By His knowledge the deeps were broken up and the skies drip with dew" (3:19-20). This echoes the point that was made in the section titled *The Timeless Nature of Wisdom* (pp. 22-26). Wisdom existed with God from before the Creation and was used by Him in creating the heavens and earth (8:22-29).

"My son, let them not vanish from your sight; keep sound wisdom and discretion" (3:21). The father appeals to his son to keep hold of godly wisdom and understanding. It is not enough for his son to just listen and learn; he also needs to *retain* what he learned.

"So they will be life to your soul and adornment to your neck" (3:22). The father is encouraging his son to be clothed with wisdom and discretion. These teachings are to be *"a graceful wreath to* [his] *head and ornaments about* [his] *neck"* (1:9). In speaking of Wisdom, the father tells his son: *"Prize her, and she will exalt you; she will honor you if you embrace her. She will place on your head a garland of grace; she will present you with a crown of beauty"* (4:8-9). As one is *clothed* with wisdom and discretion, he obtains *life* for his soul (cf. 12:28).

"Then you will walk in your way securely and your foot will not stumble" (3:23). One of the benefits of wisdom is the security and stability that one enjoys in life, as opposed to the volatile and uncertain life of one who rejects divine wisdom. *"He who walks in integrity walks securely, but he who perverts his ways will be found out"* (10:9).

***"When you lie down, you will not be afraid; when you lie down, your sleep will be sweet"* (3:24).** This verse mentions two benefits of wisdom. First, wisdom offers *security* [see previous verse]. Second, following after divine wisdom allows one to have a good conscience, thus making his sleep *sweet*.

***"Do not be afraid of sudden fear nor of the onslaught of the wicked when it comes; for the Lord will be your confidence and will keep your foot from being caught"* (3:25-26).** Even though one may be walking according to God's wisdom, there will be enemies that will rise up. However, if we follow after wisdom, we should take courage. There is *strength* in wisdom. *"A wise man is strong, and a man of knowledge increases power"* (24:5). *"A wise man scales the city of the mighty and brings down the stronghold in which they trust"* (21:22). Why is there such strength in wisdom? It is because this wisdom comes from the Lord. He is our *confidence*. As long as we stand with Him, we can be assured of triumph.

* * *

> *"For wisdom will enter your heart and knowledge will be pleasant to your soul; discretion will guard you, understanding will watch over you, to deliver you from the way of evil, from the man who speaks perverse things; from those who leave the paths of uprightness to walk in the ways of darkness; who delight in doing evil and rejoice in the perversity of*

evil; whose paths are crooked, and who are devious in their ways; to deliver you from the strange woman, from the adulteress who flatters with her words; that leaves the companion of her youth and forgets the covenant of her God; for her house sinks down to death and her tracks lead to the dead; none who go to her return again, nor do they reach the paths of life.

"So you will walk in the way of good men and keep to the paths of the righteous. For the upright will live in the land and the blameless will remain in it; but the wicked will be cut off from the land and the treacherous will be uprooted from it" (2:10-22).

Wisdom not only provides us with blessings for following it, but it also delivers us from evil. This is, of course, if we store up wisdom. Just before the passage above, the wise man says, *"He stores up sound wisdom for the upright; He is a shield to those who walk in integrity"* (2:7). The protection that comes with wisdom can only be realized if we pursue it. So these verses that talk about wisdom delivering us from evil assume that we have first *acquired* it. We will discuss the *acquisition* of wisdom later in the study. But understanding these benefits of wisdom shows us *why* we should work to acquire it.

***"For wisdom will enter your heart and knowledge will be pleasant to your soul; discretion will guard you, understanding will watch over you"* (2:10-11).** A superficial knowledge of the instructions of the wise will not deliver us from anything. Wisdom must enter our hearts and souls if we want it to guard and watch over us. Therefore, we must be *"attentive to wisdom"* (2:2) and retain it in our innermost being. Only then can be expect wisdom to deliver us from evil and prevent us from doing things we will later regret.

"To deliver you from the way of evil, from the man who speaks perverse things; from those who leave the paths of uprightness to walk in the ways of darkness; who delight in doing evil and rejoice in the perversity of evil; whose paths are crooked, and who are devious in their ways" **(2:12-15).** In delivering us *"from the way of evil,"* wisdom is designed to protect us from the influence of those who would lead us in the *"way of evil."* The first of these that the wise man mentions is *"the man who speaks perverse things."* This is the man who will try to lead us into sin by false teaching, lies, or verbal attacks. Second, we are warned about *"those who leave the paths of uprightness."* They take pleasure in doing evil and will deviously try to lead others to follow after them. We are not to follow them or fall prey to them.

"To deliver you from the strange woman, from the adulteress who flatters with her words; that leaves the companion of her youth and forgets the covenant of her God; for her house sinks down to death and her tracks lead to the dead; none who go to her return again, nor do they reach the paths of life" **(2:16-19).** Wisdom also helps to deliver us from the dangers of the *"strange woman,"* or the *"adulteress."* Much more attention is given to her later in the book of Proverbs (5:1-14; 6:24-35; 7:1-27; 9:13-18), and we will consider her more in a different part of our study. But we are told here that by following wisdom, we can avoid the ruin and damnation that comes from following the adulteress.

"So you will walk in the way of good men and keep to the paths of the righteous" **(2:20).** If we avoid the *"way of evil"* (2:12) and those who would lead us down that path,

naturally we should expect to *"walk in the way of good men."* We are going to keep company with one group of people – either the righteous or the wicked. Wisdom and righteousness are inseparable from one another. As wisdom delivers us from evil, it leads us in *"the paths of the righteous."*

"For the upright will live in the land and the blameless will remain in it; but the wicked will be cut off from the land and the treacherous will be uprooted from it" (2:21-22). The wise man reminds us at the end of this section of God's blessings and punishment. Those who through the instructions of wisdom live uprightly will be blessed. Those who reject wisdom and pursue wickedness will be rooted up.

* * *

> *"Where there is no vision, the people are unrestrained, but happy is he who keeps the law"* (29:18).

The *vision* to which the wise man refers is the *revelation* (NKJV) that comes down from above, instructing us in godly wisdom. Without God's instructions, man is *"unrestrained."* Without His standard, there is no real standard for man to follow. While many foolishly believe that the absence of a divine standard is desirable, following the *"way which seems right to a man"* only leads to *"death"* (14:12; 16:25). One is *happy*, or blessed, if he *"keeps the law"* that has been delivered by divine revelation. Pursuing God's wisdom is for our benefit. Therefore, we must *trust God* and not ourselves and follow Him in all things.

"Trust in the Lord with all your heart and do not lean on your own understanding. In all your ways acknowledge Him, and He will make your paths straight. Do not be wise in your own eyes; fear the Lord and turn away from evil. It will be healing to your body and refreshment to your bones" (3:5-8).

The Perils of Wickedness

After considering the value of wisdom, the rewards of wisdom, and the deliverance from evil that wisdom provides, we will next consider the *perils of wickedness* to further reinforce what we have already learned: embracing and following the wisdom that comes from above is for our good.

The *perils of wickedness* can be divided into three categories: hardship in life, lack of hope for the future, and the inevitability of judgment.

"Good understanding produces favor, but the way of the treacherous is hard" (13:15).

The first peril of wickedness is *hardship in life*. People often complain about the way of God being difficult to follow. In one sense it is (cf. Matthew 7:13-14), but the path of wickedness contains hardships that can be avoided if one will simply follow what is right. The hardships that come as a result of one rejecting God's wisdom are unnecessary and avoidable.

"His own iniquities will capture the wicked, and he will be held with the cords of his sin. He will die for lack of instruction, and in the greatness of his folly he will go

astray" **(5:22-23).** One of the lies of sin is to convince us that we are still in control, rather than sin becoming master over us. But sins (*iniquities*) capture, or bind, us. Paul later wrote, *"Do you not know that when you present yourselves to someone as slaves for obedience, you are slaves of the one whom you obey, either of sin resulting in death, or of obedience resulting in righteousness?"* (Romans 6:16). When we pursue sin, rather than righteousness or divine wisdom, we become *slaves* of sin. The end result is that we *"die for lack of instruction."* This shows us that God's *instruction* teaches us to repudiate sin. Many believe that sin is tolerable because it cannot cause a child of God to be lost. This idea is false. The word of God plainly teaches us to avoid sin (cf. Titus 2:12). Therefore, if one ignores this instruction and chooses to live without it, he will be captured by his iniquities, which will ultimately result in death – either physical death (as is Solomon's primary point) or, as we extend the application, spiritual death (Romans 6:23).

"A worthless person, a wicked man, is the one who walks with a perverse mouth, who winks with his eyes, who signals with his feet, who points with his fingers; who with perversity in his heart continually spreads strife. Therefore his calamity will come suddenly; instantly he will be broken and there will be no healing" **(6:12-15).** The actions described here refer to one who is a troublemaker and intent upon spreading strife among brethren. When one acts corruptly like this, the wise man says that his calamity that will result from his wickedness will be unexpected, coming *suddenly* and *instantly*. He may be able to deceive himself into thinking there is no cause for concern – and many who follow after wickedness will do this, causing their own consciences to become *seared* (1 Timothy 4:2) – but trouble will eventually come for him.

"If you are wise, you are wise for yourself, and if you scoff, you alone will bear it" **(9:12).** This reminds us of the principle of *personal responsibility*. When one rejects divine wisdom and acts wickedly, he will not be able to blame anyone else for his actions or the consequences of those actions.

"When a wicked man comes, contempt also comes, and with dishonor comes scorn" **(18:3).** As one rejects God's wisdom and follows after sin, he becomes known by others for his character and his actions. Though one may believe he will help *himself* by engaging in sin (and all sin is fundamentally rooted in selfishness), his actions will produce a reputation about him; and that reputation will result in dishonor and contempt. He will be seen as *"an abomination to men"* (24:8-9).

"Also it is not good for a person to be without knowledge, and he who hurries his footsteps errs. The foolishness of man ruins his way, and his heart rages against the Lord" **(19:2-3).** Rejecting truth and wisdom is rebellion against God. This leads to *ruin* for the one who rejected wise counsel. This is why *"it is not good for a person to be without knowledge."* Therefore, instead of *hurrying* to act, which often causes one to *err* from the truth and suffer the consequences, it is good to stop in order to listen, consider, and learn. It is the same principle that James emphasized: *"Everyone must be quick to hear, slow to speak and slow to anger; for the anger of man does not achieve the righteousness of God"* (James 1:19-20).

"The sacrifice of the wicked is an abomination, how much more when he brings it with evil intent!" **(21:27).** Besides being *"an abomination to men"* (24:9), the wicked man is an abomination to God. Further, his *"sacrifice...is an abomination."* God will not be pleased with what he offers and will not

accept him. No amount of sacrifice will please God when it comes from one who refuses to obey Him. Samuel told Saul, *"Has the Lord as much delight in burnt offerings and sacrifices as in obeying the voice of the Lord? Behold, to obey is better than sacrifice"* (1 Samuel 15:22). The wicked man being discussed in this verse is not penitent; he continues to rebel against God and choose his own way over the paths of wisdom. Therefore, his sacrifice is an abomination to God. Any *"evil intent"* in his heart only compounds the problem.

"A man who is laden with the guilt of human blood will be a fugitive until death; let no one support him" (28:17). Time does not bring forgiveness. Unless and until one meets the divine condition for forgiveness (repentance), his sins are still held against him, no matter how much time has passed. The wise man encourages us to not support such a one who is in sin and refuses to repent. Of course, we should be ready to help turn him back to the truth if possible (11:30); but as long as he remains in his sin, he is worthy of no support.

* * *

> *"Do not fret because of evildoers or be envious of the wicked; for there will be no future for the evil man; the lamp of the wicked will be put out"* (24:19-20).

The second peril of wickedness is a *lack of hope for the future*. Any "benefit" that comes from following wickedness and worldly wisdom is only temporary. The Hebrew writer talked about Moses who forsook *"the passing pleasures of sin"* (Hebrews 11:25). While sin may seem appealing, it is certainly *passing*. There are no long-term benefits for sin.

"He who troubles his own house will inherit wind, and the foolish will be servant to the wisehearted" **(11:29).** The Bible reminds us that we reap what we sow (Galatians 6:7). The prophet Hosea said, *"For they sow the wind and they reap the whirlwind"* (Hosea 8:7). For all the effort of the wicked man, his labors are only futile and destructive. Those who are closest to him (*"his own house"*) will also have to suffer the consequences of his actions. The wise man then tells of the foolish serving the wise, pointing to the future exaltation of the righteous and humbling of the wicked. He says elsewhere: *"The evil will bow down before the good, and the wicked at the gates of the righteous"* (14:19).

"A man who wanders from the way of understanding will rest in the assembly of the dead" **(21:16).** This verse does not address those who never learned God's word. Instead, it is about those who are taught the truth, understand it, and then forsake it. Despite once being *in* the way of understanding, the one who rejects and leaves the truth has a future of damnation awaiting him if he does not return to the truth.

"He who sows iniquity will reap vanity, and the rod of his fury will perish" **(22:8).** We have already noticed the principle that we reap what we sow (11:29). When one sows the seeds of sin, what might we expect him to reap? There are certainly consequences in this life (13:15) and the next (Romans 6:23). But instead of focusing on these consequences, the wise man emphasizes the utter futility of sinful pursuits. The seeds of sin, when sown, will reap only that which is vain. *"The rod of his fury"* – his power to do evil – will perish. Anything that is of lasting value comes from one faithfully obeying God and seeking the wisdom that comes from above.

***"Do not fret because of evildoers or be envious of the wicked; for there will be no future for the evil man; the lamp of the wicked will be put out"* (24:19-20).** After noting the fact that the wicked have no future to which they can look forward, Solomon tells us not to fret (worry) over them or envy them. It can be easy to worry and envy when we are too short-sighted to look at matters that extend past this life. Even if we see the wicked prosper in this life, we should not fret over them or envy them. No amount of prosperity in this life can compare to the great worth of the reward promised to those who will be faithful to the Lord (Matthew 16:26).

***"When the wicked increase, transgression increases; but the righteous will see their fall"* (29:16).** Wickedness tends to progress *"from bad to worse"* (2 Timothy 3:13). Sin leads to more sin, which leads to increasingly more difficulties and destruction. But we have a two-fold assurance at the end of this verse. First, the wicked *will* fall. The "benefits" they enjoy from their sins are only temporary. Second, the righteous will *see* the fall of the wicked, implying that the righteous will be spared and will have a future after judgment comes against those who are wicked.

* * *

"Judgments are prepared for scoffers, and blows for the back of fools" (19:29).

The third peril of wickedness is the *inevitability of judgment*. Judgment comes in various forms. One can be judged through the word of God as he is reproved by it (Hebrews 4:12). One can be judged in that he suffers the physical consequences of his error. One may also be judged by civil authorities when his wickedness is manifested in his violation of a just law. Finally, one stands to face God in judgment and receive punishment if his deeds are evil.

***"On the lips of the discerning, wisdom is found, but a rod is for the back of him who lacks understanding"* (10:13).** The *rod* is a symbol of corrective discipline and is used throughout the book of Proverbs (13:24; 14:3; 22:15; 23:13-14; 26:3; 29:15). One who is *discerning* and displays *wisdom* does not need such correction. One who rejects wisdom and instruction must receive the *rod* in order to convince him to repent. This corrective discipline, when administered appropriately, is a sign that one has been judged as having transgressed the standard of righteousness.

***"A rebellious man seeks only evil, so a cruel messenger will be sent against him"* (17:11).** The *"cruel messenger"* would be one to teach him his lesson for his rebelliousness. This could be done through corrective discipline (cf. 10:13) or through experience as he sees the negative consequences of his behavior. In either case, one who is rebellious must learn that his ways are evil. Therefore, judgments must be made against him.

***"A man of great anger will bear the penalty, for if you rescue him, you will only have to do it again"* (19:19).** This verse warns us not to waste too much of our time helping those who demonstrate that they have no interest in following the way of truth. There are *penalties* to be paid for sin. (In this case, the sin that is specified is *"great anger"*; but the principle extends to other sins as well.) Each one will suffer for his own sin. If we attempt to save someone – not by turning him away from sin but by trying to remove the negative consequences for his sin – he will continue to pursue sin and will only need to be rescued again. The judgments that come on account of sin will continue to come as long as one remains unrepentant. Besides the futility of trying to teach one who has no desire to do what is right, we must also be warned about this man's condition. We need to recognize the hopeless and miserable position of the wicked man so that we will not be tempted to follow after him to do evil.

"Like snow in summer and like rain in harvest, so honor is not fitting for a fool" (26:1). "Like one who binds a stone in a sling, so is he who gives honor to a fool" (26:8). Rather than allowing the fool to suffer the consequences of his choice to reject God and His wisdom, many try to "shield" those who act foolishly and wickedly from reality. This sometimes seems natural when one does not want to hurt someone's feelings. But these verses describe a step that goes beyond that. More than shielding one from consequences, many try to *bestow honor* upon one who is a fool. Such honor is completely out of place and unhelpful. This is the point of the illustration in verse 8. The word *stone* signifies a "building stone." A *sling* is from a word meaning "stone heap." Thus, the idea is of taking a stone that is good and useful for construction and discarding it into a rock pile, such that it becomes covered and unable to be retrieved and used. The good building stone does not belong lodged in the rock pile. In the same way, *honor* does not belong with the fool. Instead, as we have noticed in this portion of our study, hardship, discipline, and judgment belong with the fool.

* * *

Those who foolishly follow the path of wickedness will suffer for it. There will be hardships in life. They will have no hope for the future. Those who are wicked stand to face divine judgment – both in this life and beyond – for their wickedness. In the end, it is far better for one to walk in wisdom than to walk after his own way.

The Appreciation of Wisdom

Contrast Between the Righteous and the Wicked

To further emphasize the need for us to *appreciate* wisdom, we will turn our attention now to various passages in the book of Proverbs that highlight the contrast between the righteous and the wicked. We can divide these into two categories: *physical* consequences and *spiritual* consequences. As we consider the following passages, there will be a few that may have application to *both* physical and spiritual consequences; but for our study they will be placed in one category or the other.

Physical Consequences

> "What the wicked fears will come upon him, but the desire of the righteous will be granted" (10:24).

Our future is made up of three things: what we desire, what we fear, and what we do not expect. Generally, the righteous can expect some measure of blessing from God for following His will. The wicked can look forward to those things which he fears as the negative consequences for his foolish behavior.

> "The integrity of the upright will guide them, but the crookedness of the treacherous will destroy them.

> *Riches do not profit in the day of wrath, but righteousness delivers from death. The righteousness of the blameless will smooth his way, but the wicked will fall by his own wickedness. The righteousness of the upright will deliver them, but the treacherous will be caught by their own greed. When a wicked man dies, his expectation will perish, and the hope of strong men perishes. The righteous is delivered from trouble, but the wicked takes his place"* (11:3-8).

The underlying theme of the above verses is the right way and the wrong way to gain wealth. The righteous man – being guided by his integrity (11:3), understanding the limitations of riches (11:4), and acting blamelessly (11:5) and uprightly (11:6) – will avoid trouble in regard to the riches of this life (11:8). In contrast, the wicked man will be crooked (11:3) in his desire to accumulate wealth. Morality or integrity do not matter because in his greed (11:6); all he has to hope for are the riches of this life (11:7). However, his riches will not profit him when the time comes to suffer the consequences of his misplaced priorities and corrupt practices (11:4).

> *"The merciful man does himself good, but the cruel man does himself harm. The wicked earns deceptive wages, but he who sows righteousness gets a true reward. He who is steadfast in righteousness will attain life, and he who pursues evil will bring about his own death"* (11:17-19).

These verses emphasize the way in which we treat others. Those who are *merciful* and *righteous* toward others will have a reward. Those who are *cruel*, *wicked*, and *evil* in the treatment of others will suffer. The wicked man, though, *deceives* himself, thinking that he will do himself good by mistreating others. In the short term, this may work out for him. But in the long term, it does not. This is why Solomon says, *"The wicked earns deceptive wages."* He fools himself into thinking that the short term "benefit" he gets from cheating others is sustainable over the long term. It is not. Jesus would later discuss how we are to treat others when He instituted what we commonly call the "Golden Rule": *"In everything, therefore, treat people the same way you want them to treat you, for this is the Law and the Prophets"* (Matthew 7:12).

> *"A man will be praised according to his insight, but one of perverse mind will be despised"* (12:8).

Those who pursue the wisdom that comes from above will gain *insight*. With this comes praise from those who respect God and His wisdom. The *"one of perverse mind"* is he who rejects God's wisdom and walks according to his own way. Those who follow this wisdom, whether through rebelliousness or ignorance, will be *despised* by those who recognize and respect divine wisdom.

> *"The light of the righteous rejoices, but the lamp of the wicked goes out"* (13:9).

Light is used to symbolize insight and understanding. It also provides one with a sense of safety and security. The word *rejoices* is derived from a word meaning *to brighten*. Hence, the insight, understanding, safety, and security enjoyed by the righteous man abounds or *shines brightly*. In contrast, the wicked man's lamp (his understanding, insight, safety, and security) is put out.

> *"The one who despises the word will be in debt to it, but the one who fears the commandment will be rewarded. The teaching of the wise is a foundation of life, to turn aside from the snares of death. Good understanding produces favor, but the way of the treacherous is hard"* (13:13-15).

One who fears the Lord and His word, follows the teachings of the wise, and practices righteousness will be rewarded with life and favor. But the one who despises the word of the Lord and walks treacherously will suffer hardships in this life that could have been avoided if he would have just followed the will of God. Several passages make this same point. *"He who diligently seeks good seeks favor, but he who seeks evil, evil will come to him"* (11:27). *"No harm befalls the righteous, but the wicked are filled with trouble"* (12:21). *"Thorns and snares are in the way of the perverse; he who guards himself will be far from them"* (22:5).

> *"A wicked messenger falls into adversity, but a faithful envoy brings healing"* (13:17).

Those who are faithful in bringing the message of truth leading to divine wisdom are a benefit to all those who will hear them. The *"wicked messenger,"* besides providing no help to his audience, also brings trouble upon himself.

> *"Adversity pursues sinners, but the righteous will be rewarded with prosperity"* (13:21).

The wicked man does not just stumble into trouble. Solomon says that trouble *pursues* him, while the righteous enjoys *prosperity*. A similar statement is found a couple of chapters later: *"Great wealth is in the house of the righteous, but trouble is in the income of the wicked"* (15:6).

> *"The righteous has enough to satisfy his appetite,*
> *but the stomach of the wicked is in need"* (13:25).

Passages that we have already considered that speak of *wealth* and *prosperity* as being rewards for the righteous should not be interpreted as teaching that following God is a way to obtain riches far above and beyond what most in the world will ever enjoy (cf. 1 Timothy 6:3-5). However, there are blessings for following after righteousness. Jesus would later say, *"But seek first His kingdom and His righteousness, and all these things* [the basic necessities of life] *will be added to you"* (Matthew 6:33). By avoiding the ways of wickedness and by following the ways of wisdom, the righteous man can be assured of being blessed so that he may *"satisfy his appetite."* The one who rejects righteousness finds himself *"in need."* This concept is approached from a different angle in the next chapter. Solomon says, *"The backslider in heart will have his fill of his own ways, but a good man will be satisfied with his"* (14:14). The righteous man, in both verses, is able to be content with the blessings that come from doing good. The wicked man is *"in need"* of those blessings that are good (13:25), while having *an abundance* of the hardships that come as a consequence of his wickedness (14:14).

> *"For a righteous man falls seven times, and rises again, but the wicked stumble in time of calamity"* (24:16).

Even the righteous man will occasionally stumble into sin and have to suffer the consequences for it. But the difference between the righteous and the wicked is that the righteous man gets back up after stumbling and continues on in the way of truth, whereas the wicked man remains in his sin as the consequences of sin compound against him.

> *"An arrogant man stirs up strife, but he who trusts in the Lord will prosper. He who trusts in his own heart is a fool, but he who walks wisely will be delivered"* (28:25-26).

The fundamental difference between the righteous and the wicked is in whom they place their trust. The righteous man *"trusts in the Lord."* As a result, he *"will be delivered"* (this is true for both his physical and spiritual well-being). The wicked man is *"arrogant"* and foolishly *"trusts in his own heart."* Therefore, if we are to be righteous and enjoy the rewards of being righteous, we must *trust in the Lord*.

> *"Trust in the Lord with all your heart and do not lean on your own understanding. In all your ways acknowledge Him, and He will make your paths straight. Do not be wise in your own eyes; fear the Lord and turn away from evil. It will be healing to your body and refreshment to your bones"* (3:5-8).

Spiritual Consequences

While much of Proverbs deals with matters that pertain to activities of this life and our physical well-being, there are also instructions and principles that extend to our spiritual activities and well-being. We will consider these passages here.

> *"The curse of the Lord is on the house of the wicked, but He blesses the dwelling of the righteous. Though He scoffs at the scoffers, yet He gives grace to the afflicted. The wise will inherit honor, but fools display dishonor"* (3:33-35).

Besides the negative consequences that often exist for wickedness, Solomon tells us that *"the curse of the Lord"* also exists for the wicked. God *scoffs* when judgment comes against those who scoffed at His instruction (cf. 1:24-26). However, the righteous man obtains blessings, grace, and honor from the Lord. Solomon writes elsewhere: *"A good man will obtain favor from the Lord, but He will condemn a man who devises evil"* (12:2).

> *"The wages of the righteous is life, the income of the wicked, punishment"* (10:16).

This is very similar to what Paul later wrote to the saints in Rome: *"For the wages of sin is death, but the free gift of God is eternal life in Christ Jesus our Lord"* (Romans 6:23). Those who are wicked will receive what they deserve for their deeds – punishment. Those who are righteous will receive what the Lord promised as the reward of obeying Him – life. The fact that Solomon uses the term *"wages"* should not be interpreted to mean that man can somehow *earn* God's favor. On the other hand, we should not interpret Paul's statement to mean that God's grace is wholly unconditional. Even Paul spoke of the necessity of obedience to God (cf. Romans 1:5; 6:17-22; 16:26). All those who are righteous, whether in the Old or New Testament, receive the rewards of God's grace, not unconditionally, but by meeting the conditions that God put in place in the law which they are under. Even today, those who are righteous are the ones who may look forward to receiving the rewards of His grace.

> *"When the whirlwind passes, the wicked is no more, but the righteous has an everlasting foundation"* (10:25).

The *whirlwind* is often used in Scripture to denote divine judgment (Psalm 58:9; Isaiah 29:6; 66:15; Hosea 8:7; Nahum 1:3). God will punish the wicked – not just with negative consequences in this life, but with a punishment that parallels the reward of the righteous. This reward is not temporary, but *everlasting*.

> *"The fear of the Lord prolongs life, but the years of the wicked will be shortened. The hope of the righteous is gladness, but the expectation of the wicked perishes. The way of the Lord is a stronghold to the upright, but ruin to the workers of iniquity. The righteous will never be shaken, but the wicked will not dwell in the land"* (10:27-30).

Though Solomon has been pointing out many of the ways in which righteousness benefits us in this life, the rewards that come from fearing God and acting righteously are certainly not limited to this life. The *hope* of which he speaks includes hope *after* death. *"The wicked is thrust down by his wrongdoing, but the righteous has a refuge when he dies"* (14:32). *"He who keeps the commandment keeps his soul, but he who is careless of conduct will die"* (19:16). These verses make it clear that the rewards of righteousness pertain to one's soul (physical life) as well as his spirit (life after death) so that he may be secure (have *"a refuge"*) in death.

> *"The perverse in heart are an abomination to the Lord, but the blameless in their walk are His delight. Assuredly, the evil man will not go unpunished, but the descendants of the righteous will be delivered"* (11:20-21).

We have already seen that those who act wickedly fall out of favor with their fellow man (cf. 12:8; 24:8-9). But worse than falling out of favor with man is, as this passage mentions, falling out of favor with the Lord. One who is *"perverse in heart"* – meaning he has rejected God's instructions – will be *punished*, whereas *"the righteous will be delivered"* because the Lord *delights* in him.

> *"The wicked are overthrown and are no more, but the house of the righteous will stand"* (12:7).

This verse could easily be applied to both *physical* and *spiritual* consequences of either righteousness or wickedness. But more than the wicked facing hardship in this life (cf. 13:15), their ultimate future is that they will be *"no more."* This is more than just physical death; otherwise, it could be said that the righteous would also be *"no more"* at some point in the future. We can make application of this to our spirits which will live on after our bodies are dead and buried. The wicked *"are no more"* in that they will no longer have any hope or enjoy any blessing from the Lord. Those who are righteous *"will stand"* in that they will enjoy God's continued blessing and eternal reward for their righteousness (cf. 14:11).

> *"Fools mock at sin, but among the upright there is good will"* (14:9).

Sin is not just anything man might regard as being wrong. It is not defined by an individual, a culture, or a civil authority. Sin is a transgression of the law of God. Fools not only reject God's wisdom in order to walk after their own way, but they also *mock* at the very idea of sin and, by implication, their accountability before God. In contrast, the upright recognize God's instructions and the fact that He will hold them accountable. Therefore, they will follow the law of the Lord. As a result, they obtain *"good will"* or *"favour"* (KJV) from God.

> *"Will they not go astray who devise evil? But kindness and truth will be to those who devise good"* (14:22).

Those who dwell on those things which are evil will stray from God. One cannot remain pure in word and deed while being corrupt in heart. Earlier, Solomon writes, *"Watch over your heart with all diligence, for from it flow the springs of life"* (4:23). And later, *"For as he thinks within himself, so he is"* (23:7). But for *"those who devise good"* and dwell on things that are good and right (cf. Philippians 4:8), they will remain in God's favor as they continue to walk in truth.

> *"In the fear of the Lord there is strong confidence, and his children will have refuge"* (14:26).

We have already noticed that *"the fear of the Lord is the beginning of knowledge"* and *"wisdom"* (1:7; 9:10). As one fears God, grows in knowledge, and gains wisdom, he is able to have *"strong confidence"* – not in himself, but in God and the divine promises to those who are faithful to Him. This is not arrogance, as some who are *over confident* in themselves, but rather is the recognition that if one humbly submits to the will of God, he will be rewarded. Furthermore, when one is faithful to God, he will not have a guilty conscience over some hidden sin. He will not be fearfully awaiting the negative consequences that come from wickedness, not knowing when his evil deeds will finally catch up with him. Solomon later writes, *"The wicked flee when no one is pursuing, but the righteous are bold as a lion"* (28:1). With firm reliance upon God and His promises and providence, the righteous are able to be confident in the face of any situation. The wicked have no such foundation. Therefore, any time there is even the threat of trouble, the wicked man has no one to trust in but himself.

* * *

After contrasting the righteous and the wicked (both in terms of *physical* and *spiritual* consequences) and considering the value and rewards of wisdom and examining the perils of wickedness, we ought to have a healthy *appreciation* for wisdom. Having this, we are prepared for the next part of our discussion – the *acquisition* of wisdom.

The Acquisition of Wisdom

Now that we have considered the *appeal* of wisdom and can now *appreciate* the reasons why we should pursue wisdom, we turn our attention to *acquiring* wisdom. Once we know we need wisdom, how do we obtain it? The book of Proverbs addresses this question for us as well.

The Proper Approach to Acquiring Wisdom

In order to gain wisdom, we must have the right foundation. This means we start in the right *place* and have the right *mindset*, right *outlook*, and right *teachers*.

The *place* in which we must start if we hope to acquire wisdom is *in the fear of the Lord*. "The fear of the Lord is the beginning of knowledge" (1:7). "The fear of the Lord is the beginning of wisdom" (9:10). Without fearing God, there is no reason to listen to His instruction or follow after His wisdom. There is no motivation to do anything but what *we* desire. But if we fear the Lord, we will be motivated by what *He* desires.

The *mindset* we must possess starts with having good sense. This means that one *appreciates* wisdom and is willing to do what is necessary to acquire it. This is the opposite of the fool who disregards wisdom and does not want to do what is necessary to obtain it. Solomon asks, "Why is there a price in the hand of a fool to buy wisdom, when he has no sense?" (17:16). If one has *"no sense,"* there is nothing he can give in order to gain wisdom. And even if he were able to somehow *"buy wisdom,"* he would not know what to do with it once he had it. One must *"apply* [his] *mind to...knowledge"* (22:17; cf. 23:12) if he expects to grow in wisdom.

The *outlook* that we must have is one that expects continued growth throughout a lifetime. Our goal in obtaining wisdom will not be fully realized in young adulthood. Is it possible for a young man to have obtained a certain degree of wisdom in various aspects of life? Certainly. But we must be of the mind that we will continue to grow in wisdom at every stage in life. *"The glory of young men is their strength, and the honor of old men is their gray hair"* (20:29). The *"gray hair"* symbolizes *wisdom* that one has gained through a lifetime of experience. *"A gray head is a crown of glory; it is found in the way of righteousness"* (16:31). While young men might glory in their strength, they must be making efforts to grow in wisdom, even in their youth, so that when old age comes, they may be wise as God wants them to be.

The *teachers* from whom we must learn if we hope to gain wisdom must be wise themselves. *"He who walks with wise men will be wise, but the companion of fools will suffer harm"* (13:20). We cannot expect to become wise in the ways of God if we surround ourselves with those who will influence us in foolish and wicked ways. The wise man asks, *"Have I not written to you excellent things of counsels and knowledge, to make you know the certainty of the words of truth that you may correctly answer him who sent you?"* (22:20-21). The instruction from the wise man was designed to be taken and used by the one who was taught. We must have the right teachers – those who will instruct us of God's wisdom – if we hope to obtain this wisdom for ourselves. But what if one has no wise counselor to teach him? Is he then doomed to never being able to obtain wisdom? No, he can still obtain wisdom; but he must reject those who would direct him in foolish and wicked ways and follow the wise counsel found in the word of God.

And so, with the proper foundation, we have instructions to *acquire* wisdom.

> *"My son, do not forget my teaching, but let your heart keep my commandments; for length of days and years of life and peace they will add to you. Do not let kindness and truth leave you; bind them around your neck, write them on the tablet of your heart. So you will find favor and good repute in the sight of God and man. Trust in the Lord with all your heart and do not lean on your own understanding. In all your ways acknowledge Him, and He will make your paths straight. Do not be wise in your own eyes; fear the Lord and turn away from evil"* (3:1-7).

> *"My son, give attention to my words; incline your ear to my sayings. Do not let them depart from your sight; keep them in the midst of your heart. For they are life to those who find them and health to all their body. Watch over your heart with all diligence, for from it flow the springs of life. Put away from you a deceitful mouth and put devious speech far from you. Let your eyes look directly ahead and let your gaze be fixed straight in front of you. Watch the path of your feet and all your ways will be established. Do not turn to the right nor to the left; turn your foot*

from evil" (4:20-27).

The passages above emphasize the fact that wisdom is obtained through instruction that is passed from one to another – in this case, from a father to a son. We often talk about how wisdom comes with experience. This is true but not with experience *alone*. Wisdom is rooted in knowledge (3:1; 4:20). Knowledge is based upon what God has revealed (3:5-6). This knowledge of God's will must be bound about one's neck (3:3) and kept in one's heart (4:21), *"for from it flow the springs of life"* (4:23). With this knowledge, one turns from evil (3:7) and obeys the instructions of God (3:1).

Our determination to acquire wisdom must be wholehearted – trusting in God *"with all* [our] *heart"* and acknowledging Him *"in all* [our] *ways"* (3:5-6). We must remain focused, with our *"eyes* [looking] *directly ahead"* (4:25). We must be careful in our walk, watching *"the paths of* [our] *feet"* (4:26). We must be upright in all things – not turning *"to the right nor to the left"* and keeping ourselves *"from evil"* (4:27).

To Acquire Wisdom, We Must Listen

As wisdom is based upon instruction, it is therefore necessary for us to *listen* to wise counsel in order to acquire wisdom. So the wise father calls upon his son to *listen* to his words.

> *"Hear, my son, and accept my sayings and the years of your life will be many. I have directed you in the way of wisdom; I have led you in upright paths. When you walk, your steps will not be impeded; and if you run, you will not stumble. Take hold of*

instruction; do not let go. Guard her, for she is your life" (4:10-13).

Notice how the father tells his son to listen. *"Hear…and accept my sayings"* (4:10). *"Take hold of instruction"* (4:13). Elsewhere the wise man says, *"Listen, my son, and be wise"* (23:19), and *"Listen to your father who begot you"* (23:22). The goal in this listening is to *acquire* wisdom. *"Listen to counsel and accept discipline, that you may be wise the rest of your days"* (19:20).

This listening must be more than just *hearing* what is being taught. One may listen to a parent, teacher, or someone else who is trying to impart wisdom to him; but the words go "in one ear and out the other." He does not pay attention. He does not remember. And he certainly does not observe what was taught. We need to practice *real listening* if we hope to obtain wisdom. So the father says, *"Give me your heart, my son, and let your eyes delight in my ways"* (23:26). We have already noticed how the *"springs of life"* flow from the heart (4:23). Therefore, the instruction that we allow to be written on our hearts is the instruction that will have the greatest effect on our lives. So our listening must not be superficial and soon to be forgotten. We must absorb the wise counsel we receive into our innermost being so that wisdom can spring forth from our hearts to be manifested in our lives.

As we listen, we must also listen with a view toward *observing* what we learn. This is important because of the consequences of failing to do so – many of which we have already considered. The wise man says, *"He is on the path of life who heeds instruction, but he who ignores reproof goes astray"* (10:17). The wise counsel we receive must be put into practice if we hope to gain the rewards of wisdom.

> *"My son, observe the commandment of your father and do not forsake the teaching of your mother"* (6:20).

> *"For the commandment is a lamp and the teaching is light; and reproofs for discipline are the way of life"* (6:23).

This view toward observing what is taught is essential. Early in the book, Solomon writes, *"My son, if you will receive my words and treasure my commandments within you, make your ear attentive to wisdom, incline your heart to understanding... Then you will discern the fear of the Lord and discover the knowledge of God"* (2:1-5). Listening attentively, even to the point of *treasuring* commandments (and, by implication, striving to follow them), is necessary if we want to gain knowledge and grow in wisdom.

* * *

However, we must understand that there is a *right* way and a *wrong* way to listen. Let us first consider the *right* way to listen.

> *"Where there is no guidance the people fall, but in abundance of counselors there is victory"* (11:14).

Similar statements are made elsewhere in the book (15:22; 20:18; 24:6). It is dangerous to have *"no guidance."* We need to have others to counsel us in the ways of divine wisdom. But Solomon does not just talk about one or two counselors to provide help but an *"abundance of counselors."* It is good to seek guidance from multiple sources rather than putting complete trust in one man. After all, even our counselors may be mistaken from time to time. Therefore, it is helpful to receive instruction from several teachers. However, in doing this, we must heed the warning of Solomon: *"The naive believes everything, but the sensible man considers his steps"* (14:15). While an *"abundance of counselors"* can often be good, we must be careful not to believe everything we hear, lest we be like those of whom Paul later wrote who were *"carried about by every wind of doctrine"* (Ephesians 4:14). We must be careful that we accept godly wisdom and reject worldly wisdom (foolishness).

> *"The way of a fool is right in his own eyes, but a wise man is he who listens to counsel"* (12:15).

The wise man is one *"who listens to counsel."* He stands in contrast with the *"fool"* who is *"right in his own eyes."* The implication is that the fool arrogantly holds onto what *"seems right"* to him (14:12; 16:25) and is, therefore, not willing to listen. *"Through insolence* [pride, KJV] *comes nothing but strife, but wisdom is with those who receive counsel"* (13:10). The wise man, exercising humility, is prepared to listen and grow even more in the ways of wisdom.

> *"A scoffer does not love one who reproves him, he will not go to the wise"* (15:12).

The *scoffer* is one who does more than just disregard or ignore wise counsel. He *scoffs* at it or *mocks* it. He has no respect for the message or the one trying to present it. *"He will not go to the wise"*; and he will, therefore, not become wise (13:20). But if we listen with respect, both for the message and those who are faithfully presenting it, we can gain wisdom.

> *"He who gives attention to the word will find good, and blessed is he who trusts in the Lord"* (16:20).

If we hope to *acquire* wisdom, we must also listen *in faith* (trusting in the Lord). Our faith is not in the wise counselors who might teach us. As we have already discussed, these individuals may, at times, be wrong. Therefore, we must be careful to what we listen (14:15). But our faith and trust must always be in the Lord. We must listen *in faith*, knowing that what He instructs is right and for our good.

* * *

As there is a *right* way to listen, there is also a *wrong* way to listen. Let us notice a few passages that speak of this.

> *"The wise of heart will receive commands, but a babbling fool will be ruined"* (10:8).

We have already noticed that the wise are willing to *listen*. The fool, however, is not interested in *listening* but in *talking*. Solomon later writes, *"A fool does not delight in understanding, but only in revealing his own mind"* (18:2). Therefore, as a result of his unwillingness to listen, preferring to speak before he has understanding, he *"will be ruined."*

> *"Wisdom is in the presence of the one who has understanding, but the eyes of a fool are on the ends of the earth"* (17:24).

Again we see that understanding – which comes as the

result of *listening* – leads to wisdom. Sometimes the fool is unwilling to listen because he is only interested in speaking (10:8; 18:2). Other times he may listen, but he does not listen well because he is distracted. His *"eyes...are on the ends of the earth,"* and he will not focus on the instruction that can lead to wisdom.

> *"Do not speak in the hearing of a fool, for he will despise the wisdom of your words"* (23:9).

In this verse, Solomon addresses those who teach, warning them of the futility of trying to teach one who is a fool. The fool will not listen because he *despises wisdom*. Therefore, any teaching he may hear as the result of one trying to instruct him will be rejected.

> *"How blessed in the man who fears always, but he who hardens his heart will fall into calamity"* (28:14).

The hard heart belongs to the person who refuses to listen because he does not believe he needs to listen. He is stuck in his ways, refusing to change or even acknowledge that a change might, at times, be necessary. He trusts in himself and does not see the need to fear God and follow Him. Solomon warns that one who *"hardens his heart"* will suffer hardship for it and will miss out on the blessings that come from humbly listening to wise counsel.

To Acquire Wisdom, We Must Learn

Another step in *acquiring* wisdom is that we must *learn*. The knowledge that leads to understanding is available, both through the written word of God and the wise counsel that we receive from others. But the mere fact that knowledge is available does not mean we will automatically obtain it. We must *learn* it for ourselves.

If we are to *learn*, we must *seek to learn*. That is, we must have a desire to learn.

> *"The mind of the intelligent seeks knowledge, but the mouth of fools feeds on folly"* (15:14).

One who is *intelligent*, who will attain to wisdom, will not wait for knowledge to come to him. He will *seek knowledge*. We often talk about wisdom coming through experience. This is true, but it does not come by experience *alone*. We must seek after knowledge that has been revealed from God and not be like the fool who is content with *folly*.

> *"The mind of the prudent acquires knowledge, and the ear of the wise seeks knowledge"* (18:15).

We have already discussed the importance of *listening*. This is certainly found in this verse as well. But more than just listening, this verse emphasizes the need to *seek after* wise counsel rather than waiting to stumble upon it. The mind will acquire knowledge, leading to wisdom, but only after the ear *seeks knowledge*.

> *"The righteous one considers the house of the wicked, turning the wicked to ruin"* (21:12).

The one who is righteous (and wise) will consider the house of the wicked. He will see the trouble and hardship that comes as a consequence of wickedness. He will observe the *"ruin"* of the wicked. The King James Version emphasizes the fact that the wicked will be judged by God for their evil: *"God overthroweth the wicked for their wickedness."* One who is wise will learn, not just by listening to or studying from the word of God and those who teach it, but by observing the way of the wicked. We must learn from the mistakes of others because we will never be able to make them all ourselves.

* * *

Having the desire to learn is essential. But some may wonder if they will actually be able to obtain wisdom or if the pursuit of wisdom will be an exercise of futility. While the pursuit of *worldly* wisdom is futile (Ecclesiastes 1:17-18; 2:12-17), we are assured that we *will* be able to learn and gain *divine* wisdom.

> *"For the Lord gives wisdom; from His mouth come knowledge and understanding. He stores up sound wisdom for the upright; He is a shield to those who walk in integrity, guarding the paths of justice, and He preserves the way of His godly ones. Then you will discern righteousness and justice and equity and every good course. For wisdom will enter your heart and knowledge will be pleasant to your soul"* (2:6-10).

The wisdom that we are considering is the wisdom that comes from above. Because it is from Almighty God, it is able to be distributed according to His will without hindrance. James later wrote, *"But if any of you lacks wisdom, let him ask of God, who gives to all generously and without reproach, and it will be given to him"* (James 1:5). This prayer that James mentioned is not answered miraculously as it was with Solomon (1 Kings 3:5-12). Instead, it is answered as we follow the divinely prescribed way of obtaining wisdom, as the book of Proverbs discusses – through learning and practice of God's word. When we follow God's way of obtaining wisdom, we can be assured that we *will* grow in knowledge and acquire wisdom. Solomon says, *"You will discern,"* and, *"Wisdom will enter your heart."* Wisdom says, *"I love those who love me; and those who diligently seek me will find me"* (8:17).

> *"Give instruction to a wise man and he will be still wiser, teach a righteous man and he will increase his learning"* (9:9).

When one begins growing in wisdom and understanding, as long as he continues on with the same mentality and desire to grow, he *"will increase his learning"* and *"be still wiser."* Growing in wisdom is a process that continues throughout one's lifetime.

> *"The naive inherit foolishness, but the sensible are crowned with knowledge"* (14:18).

There are two groups of people who lack understanding: those who desire to gain understanding (described in this verse as *"sensible"*) and those who have no interest in understanding (those who are willfully *"naive"*). Those who remain without knowledge will *"inherit foolishness"* and receive the consequences that come with that. But those who are *"sensible"* and apply themselves to understanding the will of God *will* be *"crowned with knowledge."*

> "Wisdom rests in the heart of one who has understanding, but in the heart of fools it is made known" (14:33).

Once we have understanding, which we are told we *will* obtain when we pursue it according to the Lord's will, we *will* acquire wisdom as well. Once we acquire it, wisdom will rest in our hearts where it will be manifested in our daily lives. In the same way, the fool's lack of wisdom will also be manifested. In the second part of this verse, the King James Version says, *"That which is in the midst of fools is made known."*

* * *

However, though there is a promise that we *will* learn if we seek to learn, the book of Proverbs also teaches us that there are some who *will not learn*. Let us notice the reasons for this.

> "Wise men store up knowledge, but with the mouth of the foolish, ruin is at hand" (10:14).

Again, those who act wisely *will* gain knowledge. However, if someone will not quit talking and *"revealing his own mind"* (18:2) long enough to *listen*, he will not *learn* (cf. 10:8).

> "A scoffer seeks wisdom and finds none, but knowledge is easy to one who has understanding" (14:6).

This verse talks about one who *"seeks wisdom"* but *"finds none."* Though we have already noticed how the *desire to learn* is essential (15:14; 18:15), the desire alone is not enough. One may claim to desire wisdom, and will therefore seek after it; but if he is a *"scoffer,"* he will have no regard for the instruction that would lead him to acquire wisdom. Therefore, though he seeks for it in some sense, he will not obtain wisdom.

> *"The wisdom of the sensible is to understand his way, but the foolishness of fools is deceit"* (14:8).

Foolishness deceives one into thinking that he is actually wise. Foolishness is presented as wisdom and is regarded as such by many in the world. Yet Paul said, *"For the wisdom of this world is foolishness before God"* (1 Corinthians 3:19). In this state of delusion in which one believes that what is *foolish* is actually *wise*, he will not listen to or learn something that is contrary to the "wisdom" that he already knows.

> *"Like legs which are useless to the lame, so is a proverb in the mouth of fools"* (26:7).

> *"Like a thorn which falls into the hand of a drunkard, so is a proverb in the mouth of fools"* (26:9).

The proverb delivered by the wise counselor is able to help the one who has understanding. However, the fool, though he may know the proverb even to the point of being able to repeat it, will not get any benefit from it. It is not that he does not *know* it (it is in his mouth; he is able to speak it); it is that he does not *understand* it and cannot *apply* it properly. To him, the proverb is as legs to a lame man. Though he has them, he cannot use them properly, if at all. As he seeks wisdom, which is pleasant like a rose, he comes away without the rose, but with only the thorn stuck in his hand. Because he lacks understanding, he will not acquire wisdom; and the vain pursuit of it will only bring harm to himself.

To Acquire Wisdom, We Must Be Humble

Humility is necessary in order to *acquire* wisdom. *"When pride comes, then comes dishonor, but with the humble is wisdom"* (11:2). As wisdom comes from instruction and understanding, we must be humble enough to admit our own lack of wisdom and the need to pursue it. Without humility, we will not believe we need wisdom and will, therefore, ignore it.

> *"Trust in the Lord with all your heart and do not lean on your own understanding. In all your ways acknowledge Him, and He will make your paths straight. Do not be wise in your own eyes; fear the Lord and turn away from evil"* (3:5-7).

When we possess *humility*, we will understand that there are answers we do not have and guidance that we need. Therefore, we will not *"lean on [our] own understanding"* or *"be wise in [our] own eyes."* We will seek guidance and be open to instruction. However, it is important that we get the right guidance. So Solomon says we must put our trust *in the Lord*. Many today put their trust in parents, professors, or preachers to lead them in the paths of wisdom. While we may certainly be helped by the instruction of others (11:14; 15:22; 24:6), it is only when such instruction is in harmony with the wisdom that comes from above that it will do us any good. Therefore, our trust is not in others who might teach us but in the Lord.

> *"The fear of the Lord is the instruction for wisdom, and before honor comes humility"* (15:33).

Elsewhere Solomon writes, *"The fear of the Lord is the beginning of wisdom"* (9:10). The second part of this verse tells us that *humility* is a precursor for *honor*. Earlier, the wise man says, *"The wise will inherit honor"* (3:35). Honor is one of the rewards of wisdom. The fact that humility comes before honor tells us that humility is necessary in order to acquire wisdom.

> *"He who conceals his transgression will not prosper, but he who confesses and forsakes them will find compassion"* (28:13).

Confession of wrongdoing is an act of humility. In order to confess, one must be humble enough to acknowledge his sin and admit it to others. One who tries to hide his sin demonstrates a lack of humility that will keep him in his sin and on the path of wickedness. One with the humility to *confess* and *forsake* his sin will find himself on the path that leads to wisdom.

> *"Surely I am more stupid than any man, and I do not have the understanding of a man. Neither have I learned wisdom, nor do I have the knowledge of the Holy One. Who has ascended into heaven and descended? Who has gathered the wind in His fists? Who has wrapped the waters in His garment? Who has established all the ends of the earth? What is His name or His son's name? Surely you know! Every word of God is tested; He is a shield to those who take refuge in Him"* (30:2-5).

This is the beginning of *"the words of Agur"* (30:1). He starts with a bit of hyperbole, saying he is *"more stupid than any man."* His point is that he is *humble* and not trusting in himself for wisdom or understanding. He then acknowledges the greatness of God in creating and sustaining the earth. Because there is no one greater than God, he puts his trust in Him and His word. Even though he is *"more stupid than any man,"* he is not going to be content in putting his trust in another man who is wiser and more knowledgeable than he is. Only God's words are tested and are able to protect us from the perils of wickedness. Therefore, we must *"take refuge in Him."*

* * *

As *humility* leads to wisdom and honor, *pride* leads to destruction.

> *"Pride goes before destruction, and a haughty spirit before stumbling. It is better to be humble in spirit with the lowly than to divide the spoil with the proud"* (16:18-19).

Pride leads to one's downfall. Elsewhere, Solomon adds to this thought: *"But humility goes before honor"* (18:12; cf. 29:23). This is why he says, *"It is better to be humble in spirit with the lowly."* In the long term, it is better to be humble in order to later be exalted (cf. 1 Peter 5:5-6). However, most people tend to be shortsighted and look at the immediate *"spoil"* that is associated with *"the proud."* So they arrogantly follow the path of instant gratification. Yet in the end, as they have rejected divine wisdom, they will stumble and ultimately be destroyed.

> *"There is a way which seems right to a man, but its end is the way of death"* (14:12).

The one who is puffed up with pride trusts in his own way. He rejects instruction because he does not believe that he needs it. He is unwilling to change his thinking or his direction. Jeremiah said, *"I know, O Lord, that a man's way is not in himself, nor is it in a man who walks to direct his steps"* (Jeremiah 10:23). This is true for all men of all time. Without learning of God and His ways, we cannot find the way of life. When we reject the wisdom that comes from above, no matter what other direction we take, we will be on a path that leads to *death* (cf. 16:25).

> *"Do you see a man wise in his own eyes? There is more hope for a fool than for him"* (26:12).

The one who is *"wise in his own eyes"* is the one who has rejected divine wisdom for the *"way which seems right"* to him (14:12; 16:25). He is contrasted with the *fool* in this passage. Therefore, we must understand the *"fool"* of this verse to be one who simply *lacks* wisdom, not one who has *rejected* wisdom. Because he only *lacks* wisdom, there is *hope* for him that if he can receive the right instruction, he can acquire wisdom. However, for one who is *"wise in his own eyes,"* in his arrogance he sees no need to listen, learn, or acquire godly wisdom, even though his deficiency of wisdom will be apparent to others. Solomon offers two examples to illustrate this point. *"The sluggard is wiser in his own eyes than seven men who can give a discreet answer"* (26:16). Though the impoverished and miserable condition of the sluggard is apparent to those who know him, in his arrogance he cannot see the need to change anything about his life. *"The rich man is wise in his own eyes, but the poor who has understanding sees through him" (28:11). The rich man of this verse is not a righteous man who happens to be blessed with riches. He is a rich man who puts his trust in riches. This rich man may believe that he is fully self-sufficient and that his prosperity is a sign that he has more than enough wisdom on his own and needs no wisdom from God. Yet the poor man who has understanding (divine wisdom) will be able to see the folly of the rich man's arrogance.

> "There is a kind who is pure in his own eyes, yet is not washed from his filthiness. There is a kind—oh how lofty are his eyes! And his eyelids are raised in arrogance" (30:12-13).

Arrogance causes the filthy man (one who is mired in sin) to believe he is pure. The New American Standard version uses the term *kind* with the singular *his*, suggesting an individual. The King James Version uses the term *generation* and *their*, which would indicate a larger group. In either case, the point is about those who will not listen to others who could provide them with wise counsel, whether it is the younger generation refusing to listen to the older generation, or an individual refusing to listen to others who could instruct him. Those who are arrogant will not listen to rebuke and will remain in their sin.

To Acquire Wisdom, We Must Be Disciplined

A willingness to listen, desire to learn, and spirit of humility are essential for one to be able to *acquire* wisdom. But there is one more component that is necessary – *discipline*. The instruction which we *listen to, learn,* and receive in *humility* will get us on the path of wisdom. *Discipline* keeps us on the right path once we are on it. If we ever stray from the path, *discipline* is what gets us back on track. So the wise man says, *"Apply your heart to discipline and your ears to words of knowledge"* (23:12).

> *"My son, do not reject the discipline of the Lord or loathe His reproof, for whom the Lord loves He reproves, even as a father corrects the son in whom he delights"* (3:11-12).

Discipline is not pleasant when it is being administered. The discipline of the Lord often comes to us today in the form of rebuke and correction from His word and the negative consequences that come as a result of our disobedience. We are not to *reject* or *loathe* it. The reason why the Lord disciplines us is not because He *hates* us, but because He *loves* us and wants to guide us to the way that is right. The Hebrew writer explained this passage when he discussed the suffering those brethren were experiencing at the hands of wicked men (Hebrews 12:5-10). We are disciplined because we have a loving Father in heaven who is committed to raising us properly. The Hebrew writer added: *"All discipline for the moment seems not to be joyful, but sorrowful; yet to those who have been trained by it, afterwards it yields the peaceful fruit of righteousness"* (Hebrews 12:11). Ultimately, this discipline is for our good, even though it may not seem to be from a short-sighted perspective. This is why Solomon says elsewhere, *"A wise son accepts his father's discipline, but a scoffer does not listen to rebuke"* (13:1).

> *"He who neglects discipline despises himself, but he who listens to reproof acquires understanding"* (15:32).

We have just noticed that discipline is not pleasant but is necessary and, ultimately, for our good (Hebrews 12:11). The reason why it is good for us is that through discipline we gain understanding which leads to wisdom. One who tries to avoid discipline may do so in an effort to preserve himself; but if we look into the future, *discipline* leads us to the blessings of wisdom. One who rejects discipline is not helping himself but is harming himself, thereby showing that he *"despises himself."*

> *"A slave will not be instructed by words alone; for though he understands, there will be no response"* (29:19).

The slave was one who was obligated to obey his master's instructions in all things. In this way, it is an appropriate comparison to our responsibility to obey the Lord. There must be more than just *teaching* (*"words alone"*); otherwise, what is there to motivate the slave to obey? Even if the slave hears the instructions and understands them, there is no reason to obey the instructions without the threat of real consequences for disobedience – *discipline*. Discipline is necessary to motivate one who knows what is right to actually do it.

* * *

Though discipline is necessary for one to learn, many do not see the point of trying to learn. The book of Proverbs contains a few passages that deal with the *benefit* of discipline and the end result of it.

> *"Listen to counsel and accept discipline, that you may be wise the rest of your days"* (19:20).

The New American Standard translates the second part of this verse, *"that you may be wise the rest of your days."* The King James Version is slightly different: *"That thou mayest be wise in thy latter end."* The former emphasizes a progression of gaining wisdom while the latter emphasizes the goal of possessing wisdom in the end. In either case, discipline is about our *future*, rather than the present. In the future, the discipline that leads us to grow in knowledge from God will result in wisdom, understanding (12:1), and honor (13:18).

> *"For the commandment is a lamp and the teaching is light; and reproofs for discipline are the way of life"* (6:23).

In the previous verses, we saw that *discipline* leads to wisdom (19:20), understanding (12:1), and honor (13:18). If these were not enough to convince one of the benefits of discipline, the wise man adds here that the path of discipline is *"the way of life."* It will help us avoid trouble in this life (6:24-35), as well as in the next (7:22-27).

> *"A fool rejects his father's discipline, but he who regards reproof is sensible"* (15:5).

Knowing the benefits of discipline, it is a fool who rejects it. One who is *sensible* will accept discipline because he knows that it is ultimately for his good.

> *"Stripes that wound scour away evil, and strokes reach the innermost parts"* (20:30).

This verse mentions the unpleasant nature of discipline. Though we might be able to immediately see the point of this verse as it relates to the discipline and training of children, the principle applies to every type of discipline. Discipline is not just about punishing wrongdoing. It is also not just about suffering consequences as a fact of life. There is another purpose to discipline – *scouring away evil*. Discipline that is properly administered (and is also properly regarded by the one being disciplined) will help him to remove sin from his life, not just outwardly, but from his heart.

* * *

Unfortunately, not all are willing to accept discipline as being for their good. Some will reject it. This has consequences.

> *"Grievous punishment is for him who forsakes the way; he who hates reproof will die"* (15:10).

The way that is being forsaken is the way of *wisdom*. Those who reject God's standard and do not walk according to it will be punished. The goal of discipline (*"reproof"*) is correction so that the one who once rejected God's ways will return to them. One who *"hates reproof"* will continue on the path that leads away from life and, without an appropriate change of direction, will eventually face *death* – not physical death (which we must all face) but eternal separation from God.

> *"Cease listening, my son, to discipline, and you will stray from the words of knowledge"* (19:27).

The wise man is, of course, not trying to persuade his son

to stop listening to discipline. He is simply explaining the consequences of ceasing to listen. He *"will stray"* – indicating not a *possibility*, but a *certainty* – from true knowledge and wisdom, following instead the path that leads to punishment and death (15:10).

> *"A whip is for the horse, a bridle for the donkey, and a rod for the back of fools"* (26:3).

The whip and the bridle were necessary for these animals because they could not understand and decide to take the right path on their own with nothing more than verbal instructions from their owner. Therefore, the whip and the bridle were necessary in order to persuade them to do what was expected of them. The longer it took for them to listen and respond appropriately, the more pain and discomfort the animal would feel. In the same way, *"a rod* [is] *for the back of fools,"* in that one who rejects discipline and refuses to follow wisdom will continue to suffer the consequences of his disobedience.

> *"A man who hardens his neck after much reproof will suddenly be broken beyond remedy"* (29:1).

The hardening of the neck refers to one's heart becoming calloused. Though he may be *disciplined* in order to be corrected, his conscience has become seared (cf. 1 Timothy 4:2) so that he will not abandon his sin. Eventually, after rejecting discipline for so long, he will be broken *suddenly* (cf. 6:15), meaning his sin will catch up with him and he will reach the point of no return. This is when his *calamity* (6:15) comes. There will come a point in the future when everyone who rejects discipline and continues in the path of wickedness will no longer have any hope of correction and avoiding the ultimate fate for their folly.

* * *

The passages we have noticed so far on the topic of *discipline* have had to do with *receiving* discipline. But what if we are the ones needing to exercise discipline and reprove others? The book of Proverbs contains instructions that teach us how we are to administer discipline and warns us of how it will often be received.

> *"He who corrects a scoffer gets dishonor for himself, and he who reproves a wicked man gets insults for himself. Do not reprove a scoffer, or he will hate you, reprove a wise man and he will love you"* (9:7-8).

The dishonor one receives when he corrects a scoffer is from the scoffer himself. He is not interested in learning the way of wisdom. He simply wants to do what seems right to him. Therefore, if one tries to correct him, *"he will hate you."* Elsewhere it says, *"A scoffer does not love one who reproves him, he will not go to the wise"* (15:12). Rather than responding with gratitude, as the wise man will, the scoffer will respond with *insults* directed toward the one attempting to correct him. One must have a thick skin if he is going to correct others, or else he will soon abandon his attempts.

> *"Understanding is a fountain of life to one who has it, but the discipline of fools is folly"* (16:22).

> *"A rebuke goes deeper into one who has understanding than a hundred blows into a fool"* (17:10).

> *"Though you pound a fool in a mortar with a pestle along with crushed grain, yet his foolishness will not depart from him"* (27:22).

The first verse listed above describes the discipline of fools as being a futile endeavor. The reason for this is because the fool is not willing to listen. He is not interested in the truth. Therefore, any effort to teach him will be in vain. One with understanding has it because he has desired it and has worked to obtain it. Therefore, because of his good attitude, any rebuke that is necessary *"goes deeper"* into him and helps him to grow. In contrast, a fool has no desire to gain understanding. Therefore, the discipline that would help the wise man, though it may be administered a hundred times to the fool, will not cause any change in him. Though he may be crushed, *"yet his foolishness will not depart from him."*

> *"Strike a scoffer and the naive may become shrewd, but reprove one who has understanding and he will gain knowledge"* (19:25).

From the earlier passages, it may seem as though the discipline of fools is pointless. If they will not listen and correct their ways, why bother trying to correct them at all? The answer is found in this verse. When a person *"strike*[s] *a scoffer,"* though one may be dishonored, insulted, and hated (9:7-8), others may be helped by one's efforts. Though the scoffer may not change, *"the naive"* who witness your efforts may learn the lesson that was intended for the one receiving the discipline. As a result, he may become *shrewd* or *wise* (cf. 21:11).

> *"He who rebukes a man will afterward find more favor than he who flatters with the tongue"* (28:23).

This is another passage that reminds us that it is better to try to correct someone than not, even if we risk the insults and hatred that sometimes come from one who rejects discipline. Flattering the one who needs to change does nothing to help them. Rebuking him may result in insults and hatred (9:7-8). Or it could lead him to *"love you"* (9:8) as he learns the way of wisdom. *"Better is open rebuke than love that is concealed"* (27:5). Better to rebuke someone on the chance that he will repent than to flatter him and thus provide implicit encouragement for him to remain in his sin.

The Application of Wisdom

It is absolutely essential that we recognize the *appeal* of wisdom. Once we know that Wisdom is calling to us, we must learn to *appreciate* wisdom so that we have a reason to pay attention to her appeals. Understanding this, we then need to work toward *acquiring* wisdom. But all of this is futile if, after we do all to *acquire* it, we do not *apply* wisdom.

The bulk of the book of Proverbs, and the majority of our study, focuses on the *application* of wisdom. When God reveals His wisdom, man is not to pursue it merely out of intellectual curiosity. God expects us to put what we learn into practice.

> *"Every prudent man acts with knowledge, but a fool displays folly"* (13:16).

A *"prudent man"* does not merely *possess* knowledge, though he certainly does possess it. He will do more than just *acquire* knowledge. He will *act with knowledge*. The things that he learns will be put on display in his life, just as folly is on display in the life of the fool.

> *"Doing wickedness is like sport to a fool, and so is wisdom to a man of understanding"* (10:23).

The fool is said to *enjoy* practicing wickedness. It is like a sport to him. A contrast is made between the fool and the man of understanding. The fool enjoys *"doing wickedness."* Though *"doing"* is not explicitly stated in regard to wisdom, the contrast implies it. Just as the fool enjoys *"doing wickedness,"* the man of understanding enjoys *doing* that which is wise.

> *"A plan in the heart of a man is like deep water, but a man of understanding draws it out"* (20:5).

Water that is at the bottom of a deep well has the *potential* to do good, but only when one does what is necessary to draw it out is it actually helpful to him. In the same way, having plans and intentions to do good and act with wisdom only have the *potential* of doing good. One who has learned the truth has the capacity to act with wisdom. But he must draw it out of his heart (mind) so that it is manifested in his actions. Only then will wisdom actually benefit the one who possesses it.

> *"Like a dog returns to its vomit is a fool who repeats his folly"* (26:11).

One who will repeatedly go back to his sin and walk in foolishness is like the dog with its ignorant and disgusting behavior. There is no benefit for returning to one's foolish ways. If one had sense, he would be repulsed by the thought of returning to his folly. But the fool, like the dog who returns to its vomit, keeps going back to his sin. The instructions given in the book of Proverbs are not just for us to learn what is expected of us. They are written so that we might forsake our sin and follow after righteousness.

So as we seek to *apply* wisdom, there are several topics which we will discuss as we move through our study:

- Character – some of the more general character traits we are to have, such as self-control, integrity, uprightness, and trustworthiness;
- Speech – how we can do good and keep from doing evil with our words;
- Work – proper work ethic, rewards of labor, and consequences of laziness;
- Stewardship – making good use of our money and possessions;
- Justice – being fair in our dealings and the importance of justice in a society;
- Suffering – the reality of suffering and how to deal with it;
- Alcohol – warnings against the consumption of alcohol;
- Plans for the future – the uncertainty of life and our need to trust in God;
- Women – the value of a good wife, the burden of a contentious wife, and warnings against the adulteress;
- Family – responsibilities of parents to their children (including discipline), children to their parents, and grandparents to their grandchildren;
- Friendship – the value of good friends and warnings about evil companions;
- Neighbors – how we should treat others.
- Government – the duty of civil authorities and instructions to the citizens;
- God – His mighty works and wise revelations, as well as man's accountability to Him.

We will not cover every topic or cite every verse in the book of Proverbs in our study. But we will examine the majority of both as we discuss the topics in the list above. So I invite you to follow along with the remainder of this study as we learn more about the *application* of wisdom.

The Application of Wisdom

Character

As one learns to accept the wisdom that comes from above, the result will be a change of character. As we consider some of the character traits that one will gain from a pursuit of wisdom, let us first begin by contrasting them with the *negative* character traits of one who rejects divine wisdom. Below is a list the wise man gives of seven abominations.

> *"There are six things which the Lord hates, yes, seven which are an abomination to Him; haughty eyes, a lying tongue, and hands that shed innocent blood, a heart that devises wicked plans, feet that run rapidly to evil, a false witness who utters lies, and one who spreads strife among brothers"* (6:16-19).

Haughty eyes are an abomination to the Lord. Therefore, the wise man will be *humble*. The wise man is clear in connecting pride with sin. *"Haughty eyes and a proud heart, the lamp of the wicked, is sin"* (21:4; cf. 21:24). Pride causes one to seek to elevate *self*, while the Scriptures teach that we should be humble enough that any praise we receive is not from ourselves, but from others. *"Let another praise you, and not your own mouth; a stranger, and not your own lips"* (27:2). Pride also blinds one to his own sins. *"Who can say, 'I have cleansed my heart, I am pure from my sin'?"* (20:9). All men have sinned (Romans 3:23) and are in need of repentance. Those who deny this, in their arrogance, deceive themselves (1 John 1:8).

Therefore, we must be humble if we are to follow the ways of wisdom.

A lying tongue is an abomination to the Lord. Therefore, the wise man will be *honest*. Solomon says elsewhere, *"Lying lips are an abomination to the Lord, but those who deal faithfully are His delight"* (12:22). As *lying* is an abomination to the Lord, the *"righteous man* [also] *hates falsehood"* (13:5). One who is following after God's wisdom will not be like many in the world who are truthful when it is convenient but are more than willing to compromise their integrity in order to enrich themselves. The wise man says, *"It is better to be a poor man than a liar"* (19:22).

Hands that shed innocent blood are an abomination to the Lord. Therefore, the wise man will be *merciful*. Solomon says, *"A man's discretion makes him slow to anger, and it is his glory to overlook a transgression"* (19:11). This verse is not about one *condoning* or *tolerating* sin, but rather that the wise man will desire a sinner's repentance and be willing to forgive. Even when it comes to one's enemies, though *"men of bloodshed hate the blameless...the upright are concerned for his life"* (29:10). The trait of mercy ought to become so ingrained into one's character that he will not only be merciful to his fellow man, but will even have *"regard for the life of his animal"* (12:10).

A heart that devises wicked plans is an abomination to the Lord. Therefore, the wise man will *keep his thoughts pure*. A man's character is rooted in his heart. *"As in water face reflects face, so the heart of man reflects man"* (27:19). From the heart *"flow the springs of life"* (4:23). Therefore, the wise man will guard his heart from wickedness. Solomon says, *"The desire of the righteous is only good, but the expectation of the wicked is wrath"* (11:23).

Feet that run rapidly to evil are an abomination to the Lord. Therefore, the wise man will *seek to do good*. There are two problems with the wicked man here – his direction (toward evil) and his carelessness (he runs rapidly). In regard to *direction*, Solomon says, *"The way of a guilty man is crooked, but as for the pure, his conduct is upright"* (21:8). Elsewhere he says, *"A man of understanding walks straight"* (15:21), and, *"The highway of the upright is to depart from evil; he who watches his way preserves life"* (16:17). The wise man later says, *"Better is the poor man who walks in his integrity than he who is crooked though he be rich"* (28:6; cf. 19:1). But besides going the wrong direction, the wicked man is also *careless*. In contrast, the wise man will be *careful* and will consider how he walks. *"A wise man is cautious and turns away from evil, but a fool is arrogant and careless. A quick-tempered man acts foolishly..."* (14:16-17). The one who is in control of his emotions, however, will act with wisdom.

A false witness is an abomination to the Lord. Therefore, the wise man will be *just* and *fair*. Earlier in the list was the abomination of a *lying tongue*. A false witness is different even though they both involve dishonesty. The false witness does not just utter a falsehood, but is offering *false testimony* against another, thereby denying that person *justice*. Solomon says, *"The thoughts of the righteous are just, but the counsels of the wicked are deceitful"* (12:5). We should heed the warning: *"A false witness will not go unpunished, and he who tells lies will not escape"* (19:5). Since we will be held accountable, wisdom demands that we be fair and just in our treatment of others.

One who spreads strife is an abomination to the Lord. Therefore, the wise man will *seek peace*. There are a few warnings in the book of Proverbs that describe the destructiveness of strife. *"A stone is heavy and the sand weighty, but the provocation of a fool is heavier than both of them. Wrath is fierce and anger is a flood, but who can stand before jealousy?"* (27:3-4). *"An angry man stirs up strife, and a hot-tempered man abounds in transgression"* (29:22). *"Scorners set a city aflame, but wise men turn away anger"* (29:8). The strife that is caused by an angry man is like a crushing rock and a fire that burns down a city. But the last verse above describes the peacemaking efforts of the wise man – *"wise men turn away anger."* Though peace is not always possible, Paul later said, *"So far as it depends on you, be at peace with all men"* (Romans 12:18). One who pursues divine wisdom will seek peace whenever it is possible.

* * *

In addition to the lessons we can learn from the seven abominations, there are other character traits that one will gain from his pursuit of the wisdom that comes from above.

Self-Control

One who pursues wisdom will learn to exercise control over his emotions, rather than being controlled by them.

> *"He who is slow to anger has great understanding, but he who is quick-tempered exalts folly. A tranquil heart is life to the body, but passion is rottenness to the bones"* (14:29-30).

All men, no matter if they are wise or foolish, will encounter circumstances in their lives that could lead them to become angry. The difference is that the wise man will have control over his emotions so that he is not quick to become angry. The man without self-control will react quickly, thereby increasing folly. Solomon says elsewhere, *"A fool's anger is known at once, but a prudent man conceals dishonor"* (12:16). *"He who restrains his words has knowledge, and he who has a cool spirit is a man of understanding"* (17:27). *"A fool always loses his temper, but a wise man holds it back"* (29:11). Though the contrast between the wise and foolish is clear, it does take effort to exercise self-control. The wise man also says, *"He who is slow to anger is better than the mighty, and he who rules his spirit, than he who captures a city"* (16:32). He presents the picture of a celebrated military commander or warrior who is able to capture a city. The ability to be able to do this commands respect. However, the wise man says that one who is able to control his emotions (*"rules his spirit"*) is more accomplished than the warrior, thus showing the great discipline and effort necessary for one to exercise self-control.

> *"Have you found honey? Eat only what you need,*
> *that you not have it in excess and vomit it"* (25:16).

Self-control is not only necessary in order to refrain from doing things that are wrong. It is also necessary to control our use of those things which are good. It is true that one can have too much of a good thing. Honey is good. In describing the great blessings of the promised land, the Lord called it *"a land flowing with milk and honey"* (Exodus 3:8). But even though it was one of the good things of the land, Solomon says, *"It is not good to eat much honey"* (25:27). We sometimes hear the phrase, "everything in moderation." Of course, this would not apply to things that are sinful in themselves. But of those things that are good, we must exercise self-control so that we do not overuse or abuse the good things with which God has blessed us.

> *"Like a city that is broken into and without walls is a man who has no control over his spirit"* (25:28).

City walls during those times served two purposes. First, the walls kept enemies out. Second, the walls provided a necessary boundary, without which it would not be able to function efficiently as a city. (If all of the inhabitants and businesses of the city spread out all over the countryside, commerce and communication – the fundamentals of a city's function – would become severely limited.) Self-control works for us as do the walls for the city. It keeps enemies out (those who would entice us to sin), so that we avoid doing those things we should not do. It also provides proper boundaries for our emotions, keeping us disciplined, so that we continue to do those things we ought to do.

Trustworthiness

As one follows the wisdom that comes from above, he will also prove himself to be *trustworthy*.

> *"Many a man proclaims his own loyalty, but who can find a trustworthy man?"* (20:6).

Many are quick to claim that they are trustworthy and reliable. Yet how many actually are? According to the wise man, the number who are trustworthy is far less than those who claim to be. Man in general, as he rejects the wisdom that comes from above, will not be trustworthy. Why? It is because he has no greater standard than himself. He may keep his word when it is advantageous for him to do so. But when it seems better for him to go back on his word, he does it. The implication is that the one following divine wisdom will be trustworthy because he values *honesty* (more on this point in a later lesson) and works to build a good *reputation* (more on this point later in this lesson).

> *"Like a bad tooth and an unsteady foot is confidence*
> *in a faithless man in time of trouble"* (25:19).

This verse and the next show the trouble that is caused by relying upon one who is untrustworthy. The *"bad tooth"* makes eating difficult and painful. The *"unsteady foot"* puts one in constant danger of falling. The *"faithless man"* (one who is untrustworthy) cannot be relied upon when trouble comes. One with a bad tooth, because of the constant pain that it gives him, knows it is bad even before he needs to use it. The unsteady foot is known to be unreliable, even before the the time would come when it would be needed for walking or running. The faithless man proves himself to be unreliable, even before he is needed. When trouble comes, the untrustworthy man who follows his own way will not even be called upon.

> *"He cuts off his own feet and drinks violence who*
> *sends a message by the hand of a fool"* (26:6).

Here the one who is untrustworthy is called *"a fool,"* showing the fact that *trustworthiness* is a trait of the wise man. We also noticed that the *"faithless man"* should have proven himself to be untrustworthy, even before being called upon.

Yet some try to use such individuals to carry out certain tasks anyway, either out of ignorance of their faithlessness or in the false hope that they will be uncharacteristically reliable on this occasion. The wise man warns that one who relies upon a fool to deliver a sensitive message will only bring harm to himself.

Reputation

Wisdom also leads one to develop a *good reputation* among his brethren.

> *"It is by his deeds that a lad distinguishes himself if his conduct is pure and right"* (20:11).

The only way to develop a good reputation is by consistently doing good over an extended period of time. *"Most men will proclaim...goodness: but a faithful man who can find?"* (20:6, KJV). A reputation is not built upon words, but actions. Therefore, a lad is not going to distinguish himself by making promises or claiming to have certain abilities. He will distinguish himself *"by his deeds...if his conduct is pure and right."* When we follow after divine wisdom, we will do good. When we do what is right, we will develop the reputation of being good and reliable.

> *"The crucible is for silver and the furnace for gold, and each is tested by the praise accorded him"* (27:21).

The crucible and furnace were used to refine these precious metals and remove any impurities from them. Praise given to an individual works in much the same way. How a man reacts to the praise that is given to him is often an indicator as to whether or not he deserves it. Furthermore, one who is truly doing what is right, and not just putting on a show so that others will notice him, will live up to the praise he receives, thereby further establishing his reputation.

> *"A good name is to be more desired than great wealth, favor is better than silver and gold"* (22:1).

The wise man reminds us how valuable a good reputation can be. Silver and gold can be obtained, even by wicked men. This wealth can also be lost through no fault of the one who possesses it. Yet one's *"good name"* cannot be lost as long as he maintains it. This *"good name"* comes as the result of consistently doing good and following after the wisdom that comes from above. Nothing that is of this world (even silver and gold) can compare with that. We must be sure our priorities are in order and work on establishing a good reputation based upon good works, rather than placing our focus on obtaining the perishable wealth of this world.

Contentment

Following after the wisdom that comes from above, as it helps one to realize what is truly important, will lead to *contentment*.

> *"A sated man loathes honey, but to a famished man any bitter thing is sweet"* (27:7).

We have already noticed the fact that honey is good, provided that it is consumed in moderation [see comments on 25:16]. However, one who is so full and has more than enough will begin to loathe something as desirable as honey. On the other hand, one who is famished and does not have the abundant wealth that others have will be more grateful for the few blessings he does have and will learn to be content with them.

> *"Like a bird that wanders from her nest, so is a man who wanders from his home"* (27:8).

The nest is a place of comfort and safety for a bird. It is foolish for it to wander from that place without another home to which to go. In the same way, man must learn to be content with what he has – not that he cannot work to improve his lot in life, but that he should not foolishly abandon the blessings, safety, and security he does have in order to foolishly pursue what he desires, especially when such a pursuit leaves him vulnerable spiritually.

> *"Sheol and Abaddon are never satisfied, nor are the eyes of man ever satisfied"* (27:20).

Sheol is the grave. *Abaddon* is parallel with *Sheol*, but with a greater emphasis on *destruction*, rather than just *death*. These are always open to more lost souls who would enter into them. They are *"never full"* (KJV). In the same way, the foolish man is never satisfied. He is always wanting *more*, no matter what he already possesses. He has not learned how to be content.

> *"The leech has two daughters, 'Give,' 'Give.' There are three things that will not be satisfied, four that will not say, 'Enough': Sheol, and the barren womb, earth that is never satisfied with water, and fire that never says, 'Enough'"* (30:15-16).

These verses further describe the insatiable desire of the fool by comparing it to various other things that will never be content. The leech's two daughters constantly cry for more. *Sheol*, the grave, is what we noticed previously [see comments on 27:20]. The barren womb is never satisfied, as God made it for the purpose of bringing forth children. When no children are brought forth, there is no contentment there. The earth will always receive the rain that falls upon it. The fire will never stop burning as long as there is fuel for it. The fool, like all of these that are never satisfied, cannot be content, no matter how much he acquires of this world's goods. As we follow after God's wisdom, we will naturally learn contentment because we will come to understand that all the things that the fool desires are only temporary. As Solomon says later, *"Do not weary yourself to gain wealth, cease from your consideration of it. When you set your eyes on it, it is gone"* (23:4-5). Let us learn *contentment*, rather than waste our lives in the endless pursuit of material things.

The Application of Wisdom

Speech

The next area of *application* has to do with our *speech*. Exercising wisdom is not just about what we *do* but also includes those things which we *speak*.

> *"Excellent speech is not fitting for a fool, much less are lying lips to a prince"* (17:7).

A fool will not appreciate wisdom, listen to wisdom, or grow in wisdom. This will be seen in his character (as has already been discussed) and in his *words*. One who fails to *acquire* wisdom will not speak the words of wisdom. The wise man, however, as he grows in wisdom will develop *"excellent speech,"* which will then be evident to all who hear him.

The Value of Good Words

Earlier in the study we considered the *value of wisdom* and how it is worth far more than gold, silver, and other valuable things of this life. As wisdom produces *"excellent speech"* (17:7), we would expect that the words spoken by one who has acquired wisdom would also be valuable. Various passages in the book of Proverbs show this to be the case.

> *"The mouth of the righteous is a fountain of life, but the mouth of the wicked conceals violence"* (10:11).

Good words lead to life. This can refer to the fact that one who keeps his speech upright will be blessed in this life. It is also true that one who speaks the words of righteousness contributes to the spiritual well-being of himself and all who hear him. In contrast, the speech of the wicked *"conceals violence,"* hiding the harm that comes from his destructive speech.

> *"The mouth of the righteous flows with wisdom, but the perverted tongue will be cut out. The lips of the righteous bring forth what is acceptable, but the mouth of the wicked what is perverted"* (10:31-32).

One who has become righteous by following the path of wisdom from above will speak things that are *"acceptable"* and will impart wisdom. The wicked man, because he has rejected divine wisdom, speaks what is *"perverted"* and *corrupt*. No matter how wise he thinks he is, without true wisdom, he is only speaking what *"seems right"* to him, which ultimately leads to *"death"* (14:12; 16:25). Solomon refers to the end of the wicked man's counsel when he says his *"tongue will be cut out."*

> *"The tongue of the righteous is as choice silver, the heart of the wicked is worth little"* (10:20).

> *"There is gold, and an abundance of jewels; but the lips of knowledge are a more precious thing"* (20:15).

Gold, silver, and jewels have always been valuable in the eyes of man. Solomon uses them to make a comparison with wise speech. If we take those things that are generally regarded as being the most valuable worldly possessions, *"the lips of knowledge are a more precious thing."*

> *"Evil plans are an abomination to the Lord, but pleasant words are pure"* (15:26).

There is a slight difference in the New American Standard translation (cited above) and the King James Version. The New American Standard translation has *"pleasant words"* being called *"pure."* In the King James Version however, those who speak *"pleasant words"* are called *"pure." "The words of the pure are pleasant words"* (KJV). In either case, *purity* – which comes from one learning and applying the will of God – results in speech that is *pleasant*. This is contrasted with the *"evil plans"* – the intentions of a corrupt heart – which is an abomination to the Lord. This provides yet another reminder that the fruits of wisdom – in this case, speech – are produced from one having his heart right before God.

> *"Like apples of gold in settings of silver is a word spoken in right circumstances"* (25:11).

> *"Like cold water to a weary soul, so is good news from a distant land"* (25:25).

The two verses above describe the great value of words of *encouragement*. The word picture of *"apples of gold in settings of silver"* is a symbol of the beauty and richness of words that are used to build up others. The *"cold water to a weary soul"* is used to describe encouraging words as being refreshing and even life-saving. Without good words to encourage and provide instruction of the ways of God, there is no reason for hope and no path to life.

The Consequences of Evil Words

Besides the fact that good words are valuable, using proper speech is also important because of the negative consequences that come from evil words.

> *"An evil man is ensnared by the transgression of his lips"* (12:13).

An evil man is going to speak things that are also evil. Remember: *"For as he thinks within himself, so he is"* (23:7). His evil thoughts are going to come out in the words he uses. When this happens and he sins with his lips, he will bring trouble upon himself. The wise man says elsewhere, *"In the mouth of the foolish is a rod for his back, but the lips of the wise will protect them"* (14:3). The good words of the wise man will provide protection from harm that might otherwise come against him. In contrast, the evil words of the foolish man will only endanger him.

> *"Bread obtained by falsehood is sweet to a man, but afterward his mouth will be filled with gravel"* (20:17).

It is common for people to lie in order to get what they want. When they do this, they may have the initial satisfaction and pleasure of enjoying whatever it is that they were able to obtain through falsehood. But this *"sweet"* taste will eventually change, as if *"his mouth* [were] *filled with gravel."* This could possibly refer to the guilt that one may later have for lying in order to acquire what he wants. It can also refer to the negative consequences of lying – such as receiving the bad reputation of being a liar or the threat of vengeance from the one who was deceived. Either way, Solomon is emphasizing the fact that lying in order to gain some sort of advantage is common, but it is neither wise nor beneficial in the long term.

> *"He who goes about as a slanderer reveals secrets, therefore do not associate with a gossip"* (20:19).

One of the more common sins of the tongue is *gossip*. The wise man offers some practical advise here: *"Do not associate with a gossip."* If you associate with a gossip, he will tell others of the secret things he finds out about you that do not need to be repeated to others. Even one who is blameless and upright can suffer harm as the result of gossip spread about him. So it is better to not keep company with a gossip at all. Those who follow after wisdom will heed this advice. Those who do not will continue to associate with one who gossips. Therefore, for the one spreading gossip, there is the negative consequence of losing his godly friends (as they follow the instruction of the wise man) and being left with only evil friends.

> *"He who curses his father or his mother, his lamp will go out in time of darkness"* (20:20).

One of the Ten Commandments contained the instruction for one to respect his parents: *"Honor your father and your mother, that your days may be prolonged in the land which the Lord your God gives you"* (Exodus 20:12). Elsewhere, the Law stated: *"Cursed is he who dishonors his father and mother"* (Deuteronomy 27:16). The one who curses his father and mother will be cursed himself. The phrase, *"His lamp will go out in time of darkness,"* is in contrast with the reward of honoring one's parents: *"That your days may be prolonged"* (Exodus 20:12). There are blessings for honoring one's parents and negative consequences for failing to do so. The wise man says in another passage: *"For there will be no future [reward, KJV] for the evil man; the lamp of the wicked will be put out"* (24:20). This is the fate of one who uses his speech to *curse* his parents.

> *"If you have been foolish in exalting yourself or if you have plotted evil, put your hand on your mouth. For the churning of milk produces butter, and pressing the nose brings forth blood; so the churning of anger produces strife"* (30:32-33).

Another common sin of the tongue is *boasting*. Here at the end of the chapter attributed to Agur (30:1), we are warned against boasting. Evil, arrogant, and hurtful words only lead to strife. The psalmist wrote: *"Behold, how good and how pleasant it is for brothers to dwell together in unity!"* (Psalm 133:1). Yet the arrogant man who stirs up strife does not get to enjoy this blessing. His words create and deepen the division that exists among his brethren.

* * *

The Power of Words

We sometimes hear the saying, "The pen is mightier than the sword." This concept of *words* being more powerful than physical force is similar to the idea expressed by Solomon: *"Death and life are in the power of the tongue"* (18:21). Words are powerful. The wise man shows us the power of both good and evil words.

The Power of Good Words

> *"The lips of the righteous feed many, but fools die for lack of understanding"* (10:21).

The words of the righteous do not only provide a benefit to themselves but are able to help others as well. In this verse, Solomon says their words *"feed many."* In our society, many people have the idea that to *"feed many"* requires great amounts of money and expansive government programs. Yet Solomon says *"the lips of the righteous"* are able to do this. How could such words help *feed* others? They impart words of wisdom that will help others to be more productive and self-sufficient, relying upon the blessings that God has given rather than being in need. Later in this study we will consider the Proverbs about *work* and *stewardship*. Teaching others in such ways of wisdom will help *"feed many."*

> *"Anxiety in a man's heart weighs it down, but a good word makes it glad"* (12:25).

We are all aware of how difficult it can be to deal with anxiety and worry. Some have become so *weighed down* by these that they are hindered from carrying out the regular activities of daily life. Solomon says that a *"good word"* is able to help one deal with the mental struggles of life. He says elsewhere, *"A man has joy in an apt answer, and how delightful is a timely word!"* (15:23). Often the best thing to help one get through a difficult situation is a *"timely word"* (cf. 25:11).

> *"By forbearance a ruler may be persuaded, and a soft tongue breaks the bone"* (25:15).

How might we expect a ruler to be persuaded of something? One method that may come to mind is that of *force*. Rulers understand force. They employ force or the threat of force to persuade men to do their will. Since this is what they understand, some believe that the only way to persuade a ruler is by using force, or the threat of force, against him. Yet the wise man says that *forbearance* or *patience* (ESV) may be used instead of force to accomplish the same purpose (generally speaking, however, this would not be true for every ruler). Solomon then compares this to breaking a bone. This can certainly be done with a blow or the impact from a fall. But the wise man says the same thing can be accomplished by a *"soft tongue,"* emphasizing the fact that words are far more powerful and effective than we often expect.

The Power of Evil Words

As good words are powerful, so also are evil words.

> *"With his mouth the godless man destroys his neighbor, but through knowledge the righteous will be delivered"* (11:9).

We might expect that the godless man, by his evil words, would be able to annoy, anger, or inconvenience his neighbor. But Solomon says that the evil words of the godless man are able to *destroy* his neighbor. Through lies, deception, slander, wicked counsel, and false testimony, one is able to ruin the life, and even jeopardize the soul, of another.

> *"A worthless man digs up evil, while his words are like scorching fire. A perverse man spreads strife, and a slanderer separates intimate*

friends" (16:27-28).

Solomon uses the illustration of *fire* to describe just how destructive the words of the evil man are. James used this same analogy when he discussed the power of the tongue: *"So also the tongue is a small part of the body, and yet it boasts of great things. See how great a forest is set aflame by such a small fire! And the tongue is a fire, the very world of iniquity; the tongue is set among our members as that which defiles the entire body, and sets on fire the course of our life, and is set on fire by hell"* (James 3:5-6). The strife that is caused by the *"scorching fire"* from the mouth of the *worthless* and *perverse man* is able to divide even the closest of friends.

> *"A stone is heavy and the sand weighty, but the provocation of a fool is heavier than both of them"* (27:3).

Solomon again uses an analogy which can be easily understood. The weight of the stone or sand is able to be an oppressive burden. If it is great enough, one may even be crushed by it. He says *"the provocation of a fool"* is more burdensome and damaging than the weight of the stone or sand. The fool's *provocation*, or *wrath* (KJV), could be applied broadly. But in the context, Solomon is describing the damaging *words* of the fool. In the verses before, he mentions *boasting* and *praise* that may come from one's mouth (27:1-2). He continues this thought by describing the damaging effects of a fool's words as he arrogantly uses them against others.

> *"For lack of wood the fire goes out, and where there is no whisperer, contention quiets down. Like charcoal to hot embers and wood to fire, so is a*

> *contentious man to kindle strife. The words of a whisperer are like dainty morsels, and they go down into the innermost parts of the body. Like an earthen vessel overlaid with silver dross are burning lips and a wicked heart. He who hates disguises it with his lips, but he lays up deceit in his heart. When he speaks graciously, do not believe him, for there are seven abominations in his heart. Though his hatred covers itself with guile, his wickedness will be revealed before the assembly. He who digs a pit will fall into it, and he who rolls a stone, it will come back on him. A lying tongue hates those it crushes, and a flattering mouth works ruin"* (26:20-28).

There are several points made about the power of words in the passage above. First, evil words not only *cause* strife, but *sustain* it. Evil words are the fuel to the fire. Just as a fire will die out when it has no fuel (wood), strife will die out when there is no fuel for it (the words of the contentious man), too (26:20-21). Second, words "*go down into the innermost parts of the body.*" They deeply affect the hearer and are not easily forgotten (26:22). Third, words are able to disguise hatred in one's heart, as the ugliness of an earthen vessel can be disguised when it is overlaid with silver (26:23-26). Fourth, the deceptive words of the wicked man are not only dangerous to the hearer but will cause trouble for himself (26:27; cf. 12:13). Fifth, a lying and flattering tongue is able to *crush* and *ruin* those it hates.

* * *

Other Proverbs About Speech

As we noticed in the previous section, we should never underestimate the *power of words* – both good and evil. Understanding how important our speech is, we must be sure that our words reflect *wisdom* at all times.

Speaking Truth or Lies

One area in which there will be a sharp contrast between the wise man and the fool is that the one who follows after God's wisdom will speak *truth*. The one who rejects divine wisdom (which is truth in itself) will speak what is *false*.

> *"He who speaks truth tells what is right, but a false witness, deceit. There is one who speaks rashly like the thrusts of a sword, but the tongue of the wise brings healing. Truthful lips will be established forever, but a lying tongue is only for a moment"* (12:17-19).

The wise man mentions a couple of the benefits that come from speaking the truth. First, speaking truth imparts *"what is right"* (12:17) or *"righteousness"* (KJV). Second, speaking truth *"brings healing"* (12:18). Third, there is a long-term benefit for those who speak truth in that they will be *"established forever"* (12:19). This is in contrast with the one who speaks lies. Solomon says, *"A lying tongue is only for a moment"* (12:19). Speaking lies leads to punishment; as the wise man says elsewhere: *"A false witness will not go unpunished, and he who tells lies will perish"* (19:9). Speaking falsehood will not only cause trouble in this life; it causes trouble *beyond* this life. So Solomon says, *"He who guards his mouth and his tongue, guards his soul from troubles"* (21:23). We must work to control our tongues so that we do not get ourselves into trouble, either in this life or in the next.

> *"Lying lips are an abomination to the Lord, but those who deal faithfully are His delight"* (12:22).

The reason why lying causes trouble for one after this life is because of man's accountability before God (cf. 24:12). Lying is *"an abomination to the Lord."* It is completely contrary to His nature, as He *"cannot lie"* (Titus 1:2). Lying is in harmony with the nature of the Adversary – the Devil – who is called *"the father of lies"* (John 8:44). Therefore, God opposes and will punish those with *"lying lips."* On the other hand, *"those who deal faithfully [truly, KJV] are His delight."* As a result, those who speak the truth will be blessed by Him.

> *"Put away from you a deceitful mouth and put devious speech far from you"* (4:24).

Knowing the Lord's attitude toward falsehood and the benefits of speaking truth, we ought to be diligent to put away *deceitful* and *devious speech*. Later in the book of Proverbs, Agur mentions two requests he had before he died. The first was, *"Keep deception and lies far from me"* (30:7-8). Our attitude toward falsehood should be like Agur's in that we abhor falsehood so much that we not only want it far from us, but that we keep it from entering our own mouths.

> *"A trustworthy witness will not lie, but a false witness utters lies"* (14:5).

> *"A truthful witness saves lives, but he who utters lies is treacherous"* (14:25).

The first verse contains a statement which we would expect about who will lie and who will not. *False* witnesses lie. *Trustworthy* witnesses speak the truth. The second verse mentions the consequences of the words of these two witnesses. *"A truthful witness saves lives"* in that he keeps the innocent from wrongful punishment and brings the wicked to rightful punishment, thus saving any future victims from suffering at the hand of the wicked man. The wicked man, through his false testimony, *"is treacherous"* because his words threaten all those who are true and right.

> *"Like clouds and wind without rain is a man who boasts of his gifts falsely"* (25:14).

Clouds and wind often signal the coming of rain. When these are seen by those who need rain, a hopefulness is produced as they anticipate the approaching showers. If no rain actually comes, the hopefulness turns to disappointment or despair, depending on how badly the rain was needed. It is the same when one boasts of his gifts. Hearing of these may cause one to become hopeful if the boaster's gift would be helpful to him. But if it is a false boast, it will only produce disappointment and resentment among those who thought they might be helped by the one who claimed to have certain gifts. Many people are tempted to lie about their abilities in order to impress others. The wise man will not do this but instead will be honest with others about his abilities and gifts so that others will recognize him as being trustworthy and reliable.

Carefulness and Discretion

We sometimes hear the phrase, "think before you speak." This principle is found in the book of Proverbs. Solomon encourages us to exercise *carefulness* and *discretion* in our speech.

> *"He who winks the eye causes trouble, and a babbling fool will be ruined"* (10:10).
>
> *"On the lips of the discerning, wisdom is found, but a rod is for the back of him who lacks understanding. Wise men store up knowledge, but with the mouth of the foolish, ruin is at hand"* (10:13-14).
>
> *"A prudent man conceals knowledge, but the heart of fools proclaims folly"* (12:23).

The *"babbling fool"* – one who will not control his tongue or be careful what he says – *"will be ruined"* (10:10). Those who are *discerning* will be careful to speak the words of wisdom (10:13). But the fool who *"lacks understanding,"* brings ruin upon himself because he is not careful about what he says (10:13-14). It is better to say nothing than to speak that which is foolish. So Solomon says, *"A prudent man conceals knowledge"* (12:23). It does not say he avoids speaking things which are false. We have already seen how the wise man will avoid this. But here he is discussing *knowledge*, which implies things which are *true*. Not everything we know needs to be made known to others. The fool does not understand this.

> *"He who despises his neighbor lacks sense, but a man of understanding keeps silent. He who goes*

> about as a talebearer reveals secrets, but he who is trustworthy conceals a matter" (11:12-13).

> "He who conceals a transgression seeks love, but he who repeats a matter separates intimate friends" (17:9).

Again, these verses are not talking about speaking things which are false. They are about speaking things that, although they may be true, should not be made public. If our neighbor is involved in some private sin, or he has sinned against us, it is better to address the matter directly with the neighbor in private rather than turn it into a public matter that everyone finds out about. To *conceal a transgression* is not to ignore or tolerate sin. Rather, it is to keep a private matter private so as to (hopefully) lead the transgressor to repentance.

> "He who restrains his words has knowledge, and he who has a cool spirit is a man of understanding. Even a fool, when he keeps silent, is considered wise; when he closes his lips, he is considered prudent" (17:27-28).

Carefulness and discretion in speech is so clearly a characteristic of wisdom that Solomon says that a fool who restrains his words and *"keeps silent, is considered wise"* (17:28). The reason why refraining from unnecessary speech is a characteristic of wisdom is because the more one speaks, the more trouble can be caused by his speech. The wise man even goes so far as to say, *"When there are many words, transgression is unavoidable"* (10:19). One who does not learn to control his tongue can expect to sin with his tongue. James said the tongue was *"a restless evil and full of deadly poison"* (James 3:8).

Therefore, we must take great care to restrain our words and only speak things which are good and right.

> *"He who gives an answer before he hears, it is folly and shame to him"* (18:13).

James wrote, *"But everyone must be quick to hear, slow to speak and slow to anger"* (James 1:19). It is easy to jump to conclusions before understanding a matter. When we do this, we inevitably say things that are incorrect and unwise. Therefore, the wise man will wait to speak and pass judgment on a matter until after he knows the whole picture. A few verses after this, Solomon says, *"The first to plead his case seems right, until another comes and examines him"* (18:17). If we speak without a complete understanding of the facts, we may find ourselves to have made an error in judgment, thus bringing *"folly and shame"* to ourselves.

> *"It is a trap for a man to say rashly, 'It is holy!' And after the vows to make inquiry"* (20:25).

Before we endorse or promote something in religion, we must be sure it is right. To rashly declare something to be *"holy,"* without first searching the Scriptures to see if it is approved by God, is to set a trap for ourselves. We must first *know* what is right in the sight of God before we claim that something is holy. Our words cannot make something right. Only God's word can be used to show what is right in regard to spiritual matters.

> *"The one who guards his mouth preserves his life; the one who opens wide his lips comes to ruin"* (13:3).

To guard one's mouth is to be careful in one's speech. One who is careful in this way keeps himself within the realm of God's approval, thus preserving his life. One who is careless with his speech, and therefore makes it so that *"transgression is unavoidable"* (10:19), will ruin himself.

> *"Do you see a man who is hasty in his words? There is more hope for a fool than for him"* (29:20).

The fool in this verse is not one who has *rejected* God's wisdom, but one who is simply *ignorant* of what God would have him to do. One who is ignorant still has the possibility of being taught so that he can gain understanding. On the other hand, one who is *"hasty in his words"* is not accustomed to *thinking* before he speaks. He is not interested in learning, only in speaking. As Solomon says in another passage: *"A fool does not delight in understanding, but only in revealing his own mind"* (18:2).

Teaching

One of the important things we can do in our speech is *teaching*. Solomon discusses this in the book of Proverbs as well.

> *"The lips of the wise spread knowledge, but the hearts of fools are not so"* (15:7).

The wisdom that comes from above is not intended for an elite few while others are left without it. If we have acquired knowledge, we should want to share what we know so that others can also gain knowledge and become wise. It is the mark of a fool for one to not want to spread knowledge and help others learn what they ought to know.

> *"He who says to the wicked, 'You are righteous,' peoples will curse him, nations will abhor him; but to those who rebuke the wicked will be delight, and a good blessing will come upon them. He kisses the lips who gives a right answer"* (24:24-26).

The prophet Isaiah said, *"Woe to those who call evil good, and good evil"* (Isaiah 5:20). Though there is often a tendency today for men to praise those who do what is wrong, we help no one when we call the wicked righteous. We must be willing to call sin for what it is. We should *rebuke* wickedness, not praise or excuse it. If we rebuke wickedness we will be blessed. If we fail to do this, and praise the wicked instead, we will be cursed.

> *"Do not answer a fool according to his folly, or you will also be like him. Answer a fool as his folly deserves, that he not be wise in his own eyes"* (26:4-5).

These two verses contain similar phrases about answering a fool, but there is a significant difference between them. *"Do not answer a fool according to his folly,"* means we must not answer the fool in kind. We should not respond with *foolishness*. Though it may be tempting to stoop to his level, we must avoid doing so because it helps no one and only hurts ourselves (we become like the fool). Instead, Solomon admonishes, *"Answer a fool as his folly deserves."* Rather than answering a fool in kind (with foolishness), we should respond with *wisdom*. This includes rebuking wickedness (24:25) so that others will not engage in the same sinful behavior (cf. 1 Timothy 5:20). The important thing is that no matter how foolish and wicked others may be, we must always answer with *wisdom* and not *foolishness*.

> *"An evildoer listens to wicked lips; a liar pays attention to a destructive tongue"* (17:4).

If you speak the truth, some are simply not going to listen. Often, an evildoer will choose to listen to those who will proclaim error that supports his wickedness. Paul stated this principle when he wrote to Timothy: *"For the time will come when they will not endure sound doctrine; but wanting to have their ears tickled, they will accumulate for themselves teachers in accordance to their own desires"* (2 Timothy 4:3). People will find those who will tell them what they want to hear. This does not mean we should cease proclaiming God's wisdom so that we do not lose our audience. We must teach what is *right*, whether others want to hear it or not. But we must be prepared for the reality that some will simply not listen to the truth.

> *"He who leads the upright astray in an evil way will himself fall into his own pit, but the blameless will inherit good"* (28:10).

This verse reminds us of the seriousness of teaching. If we, through our teaching, lead a righteous man to turn from God and follow wickedness, we will suffer consequences for it. We must be careful what we teach so that we always lead others in the way of truth. We will be held accountable for how we do this (cf. James 3:1). We cannot force others to accept the truth and do what is right, but we must always point them in the right direction.

The Application of Wisdom

Work

When we consider the subject of *work*, Solomon's words in Ecclesiastes provide a fitting starting point: *"Whatever your hand finds to do, do it with all your might; for there is no activity or planning or knowledge or wisdom in Sheol where you are going"* (Ecclesiastes 9:10). Our time here on earth is limited. Therefore, we must work hard in the time that we have. Once our lives here are over, there will be no opportunity to do what we ought to have done during our time under the sun. So the wise man spends a good deal of time in the book of Proverbs discussing the important topic of *work*.

The Virtue and Rewards of Work

We learn in Solomon's writings that work is not only necessary and honorable but that it also leads to blessings from God as we carry out the responsibilities we have in life.

> *"In all labor there is profit, but mere talk leads only to poverty"* (14:23).

Some seem to have the idea that some work is worthwhile, but other work is useless. It is certainly true that from a financial standpoint, certain types of labor are more profitable than others. But Solomon says that *"all labor"* is profitable. He then warns us against spending all of our time merely talking and planning about what we might do. It is easy to become so distracted by plans and dreams that we do not accomplish any actual work. No matter how good our plans or how ambitious our dreams are, they are worthless if we never do any *work* to make those plans a reality.

> *"The glory of young men is their strength, and the honor of old men is their gray hair"* (20:29).

Solomon says that *"old men"* have the advantage of experience and wisdom (implied by *"gray hair"*). In contrast, the *"young men"* have their *strength*. Therefore, Jeremiah said, *"It is good for a man that he should bear the yoke in his youth"* (Lamentations 3:27). Too often, young men in our society want to do the least that they can to get by. Perhaps they think the time for hard work is when they are older. Maybe they are hoping to figure out some "get rich quick" scheme so as to avoid the need to work hard at all. Whatever the motivation might be, young men who are striving to follow God's wisdom, rather than worldly wisdom, should use the strength of their youth to work hard, rather than follow their peers in the way of laziness and futile, childish pursuits.

> *"A worker's appetite works for him, for his hunger urges him on"* (16:26).

When God created man, he gave him a natural indicator in his own body that would remind him of the need to eat to sustain his life – hunger. Solomon says this hunger motivates man to work hard so that he can sustain himself from the fruit of his labors. One of the reasons many become trapped in the rut of laziness is because they do not feel the motivation of hunger to urge them to work hard. When laziness is rewarded or subsidized, people will continue in laziness. When laziness causes one to be hungry, people will eventually learn that they must work so that they will be able to eat. Later in the book of Proverbs, Agur mentions three things which cause the earth to quake and four under which it *"cannot bear up"* (30:21). One of these is *"a fool when he is satisfied with food"* (30:22). When one refuses to work and suffers hunger because of it, he harms himself. When one refuses to work but is rewarded for his laziness with food and the necessities of life, society is harmed because of it.

> *"The plans of the diligent lead surely to advantage, but everyone who is hasty comes surely to poverty"* (21:5).

Earlier we noticed how talking of one's plans alone, without actually working to carry out those plans, leads to poverty (14:23). The plans that Solomon mentions in this verse are not idle dreams. Rather, they are plans that belong to the *diligent*. When careful forethought is coupled with diligent effort, one obtains a degree of prosperity (generally speaking). However, many shy away from diligent, thoughtful labor, hoping instead to gain prosperity through deception, impulsiveness, or some "get rich quick" scheme. Yet Solomon warns, *"Everyone who is hasty comes surely to poverty."* He says elsewhere, *"A faithful man will abound with blessings, but he who makes haste to be rich will not go unpunished"* (28:20). On the point about diligent, thoughtful labor, Solomon says, *"Do you see a man skilled in his work? He will stand before kings; he will not stand before obscure men"* (22:29). One will be recognized and honored for his skill in his work. This skill does not come by accident but through diligence and perseverance.

> "The hand of the diligent will rule, but the slack hand will be put to forced labor" (12:24).

Solomon says that both the diligent man and the lazy man will work. Those who are lazy are trying to *avoid* work. But eventually, work is unavoidable. At some point it will become necessary for one to work for himself after those who had been supporting him are no longer willing to do so or their resources that were used to help have been exhausted. However, one who is self-motivated and is willing to work to provide for himself (rather than being forced to do so) will *rule*. As a result of his diligence, experience, and skill, he will have put himself at an advantage over one who has wasted his time in empty pursuits.

Consequences of Refusing to Work

The wise man warns us that there are consequences for refusing to work. These consequences go beyond simply missing out on the blessings of hard work. There are also *negative* consequences that come for those who refuse to work.

> "The way of the lazy is as a hedge of thorns, but the path of the upright is a highway" (15:19).

There are two paths one can take in life – "*the way of the lazy*" and "*the path of the upright.*" In context, the *upright* is one who is a diligent worker. One who is lazy tries to avoid the hard work in which the diligent man engages. Yet this verse mentions the difficulties and come from laziness. The path of the diligent man is a *highway* – clear and easy to travel. The path of the lazy man goes through a *hedge of thorns*. The point is that everything is more difficult for one who does not develop the ability or possess the inclination to work hard.

> *"He who tills his land will have plenty of food, but he who follows empty pursuits will have poverty in plenty"* (28:19).

We noticed earlier that *"the plans of the diligent lead surely to advantage"* (21:5). The path to prosperity is not short, but takes time and requires one to follow certain procedures – in this case, tilling his land so that he might later reap the harvest. Solomon says, *"The sluggard does not plow after the autumn, so he begs during the harvest and has nothing"* (20:4). Even if one realizes his mistake late in the year, it will be too late. He cannot begin planting when it is time to be harvesting. Often when one does not do what needs to be done in the proper time, he will suffer for it. *"Laziness casts into a deep sleep, and an idle man will suffer hunger"* (19:15).

> *"He also who is slack in his work is brother to him who destroys"* (18:9).

There is a similarity between one who is lazy and one who destroys. One is *actively* tearing down what is around him (*"him who destroys"*). The other is *passively* destroying (he who is *"slack in his work"*). The next passage explains how one's laziness is destructive.

> *"I passed by the field of the sluggard and by the vineyard of the man lacking sense, and behold, it was completely overgrown with thistles; its surface was covered with nettles, and its stone wall was broken down. When I saw, I reflected upon it; I looked, and received instruction. 'A little sleep, a little slumber, a*

> *little folding of the hands to rest,' then your poverty will come as a robber and your want like an armed man"* (24:30-34).

Through neglect, the field that was once fertile had become *"completely overgrown with thistles."* Through lack of maintenance, the stone wall that had once served as a proper boundary had *"broken down."* This came as the result of the property owner's *laziness* and refusal to take care of what belonged to him. The end result was essentially no different than if one had come in and *actively* destroyed these things. The consequence of his destructive neglect was that he would become poor and destitute.

The Description of the Sluggard

In order to provide motivation for one to *work*, Solomon describes the conditions of the sluggard so that we might avoid being like him.

> *"The soul of the sluggard craves and gets nothing, but the soul of the diligent is made fat"* (13:4).

Everyone has desires they wish to be fulfilled – from the basic necessities of life (the desire for food, clothing, and shelter), to various comforts and luxuries of life. One who is diligent has a way to obtain what he desires – *work*. The sluggard, because he is not willing to work, *"craves and gets nothing."* Solomon later says, *"The desire of the sluggard puts him to death, for his hands refuse to work; all day long he is craving, while the righteous gives and does not hold back"* (21:25-26). The righteous man is able to be generous because of the reward he receives from his diligent labor (cf. Ephesians 4:28). The sluggard, because of his refusal to work, will not only have to live without certain things, but his laziness actually helps bring destruction upon himself.

> *"A lazy man does not roast his prey, but the precious possession of a man is diligence"* (12:27).

Without roasting his prey, the effort that was put forth in hunting it was useless. It does no good to begin work and then not finish it. Diligence is called a *"precious possession"* because it enables one to finish the work he starts so that he might enjoy the fruits of his labor.

> *"The sluggard buries his hand in the dish; he is weary of bringing it to his mouth again"* (26:15).

This verse is nearly identical to one found a few chapters earlier (19:24). It describes the utterly miserable state of the sluggard. Even though he may be so close to completing what would seem like the most basic of all tasks – feeding oneself – he does not even have the will to bring his hand back up to his mouth. This ought to serve as a warning of the destructive and progressive effects of laziness. When one gives himself over to laziness, difficult tasks become impossible. Reasonable tasks become an excessive burden. Easy tasks even prove to be more than one can willfully manage.

> *"As the door turns on its hinges, so does the sluggard on his bed"* (26:14).

Though a door may have movement in opening and closing, because it remains on its hinges, it never really goes anywhere. Solomon says the same is true with the sluggard in his bed. Though he may toss and turn, as long as he remains in his bed, he will never go anywhere or accomplish anything, thus bringing about his own destruction. As the wise man says earlier, *"Laziness casts into a deep sleep, and an idle man will suffer hunger"* (19:15).

> *"The sluggard says, 'There is a lion in the road! A lion is in the open square!'"* (26:13).

This verse is simply about one making excuses in an attempt to justify his laziness. A similar passages reads: *"The sluggard says, 'There is a lion outside; I will be killed in the streets!'"* (22:13). The sluggard uses the presence of a dangerous lion outside (assuming this was not a contrived excuse) to justify his remaining at home, in bed (26:14), not taking care of himself (26:15), and all the while thinking that he is *"wiser...than seven men who can give a discreet answer"* (26:16). Yet the sluggard is not wise for refusing to go out and work to provide for himself – even with a lion outside. If there was an actual lion outside, the sluggard could have done one of two things: either *kill* the lion or *avoid* the lion. But he refused to do either one. Too often people tend to make excuses to try and justify their laziness rather than simply deal with the problems and obstacles in front of them. The sluggard is the one who makes excuses. The wise man will find a way to work around any obstacle that presents itself.

Admonition to the Sluggard

After describing the sluggard and explaining some of the consequences for one's refusal to work, we turn our attention to Solomon's admonition to the sluggard.

> *"Go to the ant, O sluggard, observe her ways and be wise, which, having no chief, officer or ruler, prepares her food in the summer and gathers her provision in the harvest. How long will you lie down, O sluggard? When will you arise from your sleep? 'A little sleep, a little slumber, a little folding of the hands to rest'–your poverty will come in like a vagabond and your need like an armed man"* (6:6-11).

The sluggard can learn from observing the ant. First, the ant is *self-motivated*. Though it has *"no chief, officer or ruler,"* it accomplishes the work that is necessary for it to do. It does not need to wait to be told what is required of it. Second, the ant is *prepared for the future*. During the winter months there would be no food to be found. So the ant works hard during the summer and harvest in order to have food later in the year. Third, the ant *does not procrastinate*. In the summer months, the ant begins gathering for the winter. Yet the sluggard prefers sleep over work, and, as a result, neglects to do the work necessary to provide for himself. Because of this, he will find himself in poverty and being forced to beg (cf. 24:33-34; 20:4).

> *"Do not love sleep, or you will become poor; open your eyes, and you will be satisfied with food"* (20:13).

Sleep is necessary. But work is necessary, too. In this context, one who *loves sleep* is not one who simply appreciates the benefits of sleep and understands the necessity of rest for helping him carry out the responsibilities that he has in life. Rather, the one who *loves sleep* is one who will *neglect* his responsibilities in order to sleep. For him, rest is not a way to *recharge* from work but a way to *avoid* work. If we want to be *"satisfied with food,"* meaning we have sufficient means of providing for ourselves, we must not *"love sleep"* like the sluggard.

> *"Four things are small on the earth, but they are exceedingly wise: the ants are not a strong people, but they prepare their food in the summer; the shephanim are not a mighty people, yet they make their houses in the rocks; the locusts have no king, yet all of them go out in ranks; the lizard you may grasp with the hands, yet it is in kings' palaces"* (30:24-28).

We already noticed how the sluggard is quick to make excuses (26:13; 22:13). Agur mentions *"four things that are small on the earth"* that can serve as an example to the sluggard. The *ants* are not strong, but they work hard, refuse to procrastinate, and *"prepare their food in the summer"* (30:25; cf. 6:8). The *shephanim* (small creatures that are similar to rabbits) may have been vulnerable to predators because of their size, but they protected themselves by making *"their houses in the rocks"* (30:26). The *locusts*, though they had no ruler, stuck together for their mutual protection and benefit (30:27). The *lizard* (spider, KJV) was small enough for one to catch in his hands, yet, because of its ability to get into hard to reach places, was able to find a place *"in kings' palaces"* (30:28). Each one of these had challenges that made survival difficult – particularly in regard to their inherent physical characteristics. But in spite of their supposed deficiencies, they simply did what was necessary for their survival. We would do well to learn from these four small creatures. Instead of making excuses, we should simply use the peculiar talents and advantages we have and do the work we are responsible to do.

The Application of Wisdom

Stewardship

Stewardship refers to how we use the money and possessions we have. The book of Proverbs contains instructions that help us know how to be wise stewards of those things which we have.

Obtaining Wealth

We begin our study of *stewardship* by noticing the wise man's counsel about how we obtain wealth in the first place.

> "Ill-gotten gains do not profit, but righteousness delivers from death" (10:2).

> "Poor is he who works with a negligent hand, but the hand of the diligent makes rich. He who gathers in summer is a son who acts wisely, but he who sleeps in harvest is a son who acts shamefully" (10:4-5).

"*Treasures*" that come as a result of "*wickedness*" (KJV) are not the type of possessions we should desire. It does matter how we obtain our wealth. Rather than seeking to become rich through *wickedness*, we are to practice *righteousness*. How does one acquire wealth in a righteous manner? He does so by being *diligent* and not putting off the responsibilities of life. Though many wish to do so, we cannot escape the need to work hard. Solomon says, *"He who tills his land will have plenty of bread, but he who pursues worthless things lacks sense"* (12:11). We should strive to gain prosperity through hard work, not through deception. *"Wealth obtained by fraud dwindles, but the one who gathers by labor increases it"* (13:11).

> *"He who profits illicitly troubles his own house, but he who hates bribes will live"* (15:27).

One who *"profits illicitly"* or *"is greedy of gain"* (KJV) has material things as his sole focus. The righteous man may certainly prosper. But material prosperity is a side benefit, rather than the primary goal. For the wicked man, material prosperity is the primary goal. Therefore, he will do whatever it takes to obtain wealth without regard to the consequences. This type of attitude will not only bring trouble to himself, but also to *"his own house."*

> *"The acquisition of treasures by a lying tongue is a fleeting vapor, the pursuit of death"* (21:6).

One may be able to gain some degree of prosperity through deception. But Solomon warns that such wealth is only *fleeting*. Its end is *death* because this is the limit to which one may enjoy the riches of this life.

> *"A gracious woman attains honor, and ruthless men attain riches"* (11:16).

A woman who is *gracious* may obtain a good reputation for her character. In contrast, a man who is *ruthless* may obtain riches. The word for *ruthless* is used for one who is terrifying, powerful, tyrannical and even oppressive of others. The wise man does not deny that such wicked individuals will gain wealth. However, the difference is that the wealth of the wicked is *fleeting*, just as is true with the liar (21:6).

> *"An inheritance gained hurriedly at the beginning will not be blessed in the end"* (20:21).

We have likely all heard stories of individuals who have won millions of dollars in the lottery, only to be broke in just a few years. They became rich very quickly – just as many people would like to do. But that great windfall of wealth *"will not be blessed in the end."* It will not last because the one who acquired it does not know how to handle it. Therefore, the wealth will be squandered and lost; and he will be back in the same condition in which he was at the beginning.

> *"A man with an evil eye hastens after wealth and does not know that want will come upon him"* (28:22).

Many want the rewards of labor without the actual labor. Solomon says it is a characteristic of the evil man to *hasten after wealth* – strive to obtain wealth without the labor necessary to acquire it. He is oblivious to the fact that his attitude will result in *"want* [coming] *upon him"* (cf. 21:5; 28:20).

> *"'Bad, bad,' says the buyer, but when he goes his way, then he boasts"* (20:14).

It is common to haggle with a seller or negotiate the price of an item before purchasing it. This may be fine to some degree. But we should not take advantage of others and, in essence, deceive the seller into giving us the item for less than what would be a fair price for it.

> *"He who increases his wealth by interest and usury gathers it for him who is gracious to the poor"* (28:8).

Similar to the previous verse (20:14), this verse condemns the practice of taking advantage of others. The wise man says that wealth obtained by taking advantage of others will one day be lost. The gain is only temporary. Eventually the wealth we have obtained will belong to others. It would be better to use our wealth to do good while we have the opportunity to do so, rather than try to acquire wealth for our own selfish purposes by taking advantage of and harming others.

The Wise Use of Wealth

After we obtain wealth, we need to use it wisely. There are several passages in the book of Proverbs that speak to this.

> *"Honor the Lord from your wealth and from the first of all your produce; so your barns will be filled with plenty and your vats will overflow with new wine"* (3:9-10).

The wise man reminds us that we are to be mindful of God when we consider how we use our wealth. Our service to God is to be our highest priority, as we honor Him *"from the first"* of our produce. We focus on pleasing the Lord *first*, then let everything else follow. However, we need to be careful not to interpret verses like this one as some sort of guarantee of material prosperity as the reward of faithfulness to God. Those who teach the "health and wealth" gospel will try to do this, promising people material prosperity for one's faith (which, according to these false teachers, is usually demonstrated by one sending money to their "ministry"). Even without the false guarantee of the "health and wealth" preachers, there are blessings for following the Lord. Our focus, however, must be primarily upon serving God and being good stewards of the blessings He has given.

> *"The rich man's wealth is his fortress, the ruin of the poor is their poverty"* (10:15).

Solomon tells us here that wealth is able to provide a level of protection and stability for the one who possesses it. However, this requires that he act as a good steward of the wealth he has, rather than squandering it on worthless things. But we should notice the caution contained in a similar verse: *"The name of the Lord is a strong tower; the righteous runs into it and is safe. A rich man's wealth is his strong city, and like a high wall in his own imagination"* (18:10-11). Though wealth may provide a degree of protection and stability in life, it cannot eliminate our need to rely upon God. Our trust must be in the Lord as we make wise use of our wealth, rather than placing our trust in our riches. This point will be discussed more later in the study.

> *"There is one who pretends to be rich, but has nothing; another pretends to be poor, but has great wealth"* (13:7).

The problem Solomon describes here is common in our society. Many people try to live beyond their means – they *pretend* to the rich. In order to continue the illusion – either to fool themselves or others – they must go further and further into debt in order to maintain their lifestyle. In contrast, the wise man will live within his means – *pretending* to be poor even though he is not. Not only does this help him avoid debt, but living within his means allows him to save for the future.

> *"A good man leaves an inheritance to his children's children, and the wealth of the sinner is stored up for the righteous"* (13:22).

Three things are necessary for one to be able to leave an inheritance for his grandchildren. First, he must spend a lifetime in diligent labor. Second, he must be a good steward of the fruits of his labor so that he is able to save enough to have something to provide for his grandchildren as an inheritance. And third, he must have a desire to help them that is stronger than any desire to use the money on himself. Of course, it is possible for one to be a good man and, because of factors beyond his control, not have an inheritance to leave for his children, let alone his grandchildren. But regardless of the variables and possible outcomes, a good man will have these characteristics – diligence, frugalness, and generosity.

> *"There is one who scatters, and yet increases all the more, and there is one who withholds what is justly due, and yet it results only in want. The generous man will be prosperous, and he who waters will himself be watered. He who withholds grain, the people will curse him, but blessing will be on the head of him who sells it"* (11:24-26).

The first two verses above discuss the virtues and rewards of *generosity* and contrast it with the negative consequences that come to one who cheats others. The last verse is interesting, especially in light of modern attacks on capitalism and demonization of those who engage in business and make a profit. A constant in life is the need for people to eat. Therefore, it is not surprising for the wise man to say, *"He who withholds grain, the people will curse him."* If one person hoards all the grain, those without will starve. But notice the contrast Solomon makes to this. He does not say that he who gives away all his grain will be blessed. Generosity certainly is commendable, but this verse makes another important point: *"Blessing will be on the head of him who sells it."* Just as a *"laborer is worthy of his wages"* (Luke 10:7), so also is a seller of goods worthy of his profit. We have already discussed how one is not to obtain wealth by taking advantage of others. But participating in a free market and receiving a fair price in exchange for goods that others want or need is commendable and makes one a fitting recipient of God's blessings.

The Wise Use of Our Possessions

Being a good steward does not just pertain to one's *wealth* but also to one's *possessions*. Let us notice the passages in Proverbs that discuss how to make wise use of our possessions.

> *"Prepare your work outside and make it ready for yourself in the field; afterwards, then, build your house"* (24:27).

This verse is about *time management* in making wise use of our possessions. Both preparing one's field and building one's house are necessary. But if one does not tend to his field at the appropriate time, he will have nothing during the time of harvest (cf. 20:4). Because of the patience required in allowing the natural processes in God's providence to work, certain matters are more pressing than others. If one fails to recognize this, the field that he possesses could become worthless to him.

> *"A righteous man has regard for the life of his animal, but even the compassion of the wicked is cruel"* (12:10).

This verse is often used to make the point that one of the character traits of a righteous man is *mercy*, and it may be seen even in how he treats his animals. However, this verse is not so much about *mercy* as it is about *stewardship*. Animals are valuable in agriculture (cf. 14:4). One makes wise use of his possessions by taking care of his animals so that they will continue to do what he needs them to do so that he will prosper.

> *"Where no oxen are, the manger is clean, but much revenue comes by the strength of the ox"* (14:4).

Solomon reminds us here of the value of practicality over aesthetics. Animals – such as oxen – are dirty, stinky creatures. There is also a lot of work and expense required to keep such animals. However, the reason why one would endure the unpleasantness, work, and expense of keeping these animals is because *"much revenue comes by the strength of the ox."* If we judged and kept our possessions on the basis of beauty and sentimentality alone, we would find ourselves in poverty. While such impractical things may be fine to a point, we do need to possess and maintain those things which are practical and can help us survive and prosper.

> *"Know well the condition of your flocks, and pay attention to your herds; for riches are not forever, nor does a crown endure to all generations. When the grass disappears, the new growth is seen, and the herbs of the mountains are gathered in, the lambs will be for your clothing, and the goats will bring the price of a field, and there will be goats' milk enough for your food, for the food of your household, and sustenance for your maidens"* (27:23-27).

These verses are a strong testament to God's enduring providence. Though economies may collapse (*"riches are not forever"*) and nations may fall (*"nor does a crown endure to all generations"*), God's people are still able to survive through what He has provided. But we must be good stewards of what we possess (*"know well the condition of your flocks, and pay attention to your herds"*), using our blessings to obtain the things we need. This may be done either by producing what we need for ourselves (*"lambs will be for your clothing"*) or trading with others for what we do not have (*"goats will bring the price of a field, and there will be goats' milk enough for your food"*). By being good stewards of those things with which God has blessed us, we can survive in the world He has created.

Our Attitude Toward Riches

According to the words of Agur, there is a balance which we must strike in our attitude toward riches.

> *"Give me neither poverty nor riches; feed me with the food that is my portion, that I not be full and deny You and say, 'Who is the Lord?' Or that I not be in want and steal, and profane the name of my*

God" (30:8-9).

There is a danger in having an abundance of riches because it can lead us to deny the Lord, thinking that we are fully self-sufficient without Him. However, lacking riches to the point of being in need is also dangerous because it could lead us to steal. He encourages us to be *content* – not being overly desirous of riches, but also being mindful and thankful for what we do have. This contentment comes when we understand the truth about riches and have the right attitude about them.

* * *

The most fundamental truth we must understand about riches is that they are *blessings from God*.

> *"It is the blessing of the Lord that makes rich, and*
> *He adds no sorrow to it"* (10:22).

Everything that we have to enjoy in this life comes from God. Therefore, we should always be mindful that He is the source of our blessings, as this will help us to focus on serving Him. But Solomon adds to his statement about God's abundant blessings. Not only is it true that the good things that we have to enjoy in this life come from God, but also He adds *"no sorrow with it"* (KJV). People often want to attribute bad things in their lives to God, but the wise man reminds us that good things – and only good things – are from the Lord. Though He may allow certain bad things to happen, He is not actively bringing harm upon us.

> *"The crown of the wise is their riches, but the folly of fools is foolishness"* (14:24).

One of the benefits of following after wisdom is *riches*. As we have considered already, this is not a guarantee of financial prosperity for service to God, but it is certainly true that following after the wisdom that comes from above puts one in a position to prosper.

* * *

Although riches are *blessings from God*, there is a danger posed by them if we foolishly trust in them. So Solomon warns: *do not trust in riches*.

> *"Riches do not profit in the day of wrath, but righteousness delivers from death"* (11:4).

Though there is certainly a benefit provided to one who has riches, there is a limit to their usefulness. In the *"day of wrath,"* or the day of divine judgment, our wealth will not save us. When it comes time to depart from this life, riches will not prevent our death, nor will we be able to take our possessions with us into the afterlife.

> *"He who trusts in riches will fall, but the righteous will flourish like the green leaf"* (11:28).

This verse makes a contrast between one who trusts in riches who *"will fall"* and one who is righteous who *"will flourish."* However, this verse does *not* say how much wealth either of these two individuals possessed. One may trust in riches but have none. One may also be righteous and prosper.

To be righteous does not require that one take a vow of poverty. Rather, it means that one puts God first and does His will, trusting in Him rather than in riches. One who fails to put his trust in God, choosing to trust in wealth instead, is setting himself up for a fall.

> *"The name of the Lord is a strong tower; the righteous runs into it and is safe. A rich man's wealth is his strong city, and like a high wall in his own imagination"* (18:10-11).

Earlier we contrasted this verse with this statement by Solomon: *"The rich man's wealth is his fortress, the ruin of the poor is their poverty"* (10:15). Riches provide the benefits of security and stability to those who possess them. However, as we have seen elsewhere, our trust must be *in the Lord*, not in our wealth. Safety and security are from God. Riches may be the instrument with which we have been blessed that helps provide this safety and security. But for the one who trusts in his wealth, rather than in God, his security and stability is in *"his own imagination,"* or *"in his own conceit"* (KJV). It is arrogant for one to think that he does not need God, no matter how much of this world's goods he possesses.

> *"Do not weary yourself to gain wealth, cease from your consideration of it. When you set your eyes on it, it is gone. For wealth certainly makes itself wings like an eagle that flies toward the heavens"* (23:4-5).

In these verses, Solomon is not saying that one should not work hard. We have already noted several passages in which diligent labor is commended (12:24; 13:4; 28:19; cf. Ecclesiastes 9:10). Instead, he is reminding us to have the proper perspective about riches. They are temporary and uncertain. Therefore, we cannot make riches our primary focus or put our trust in them.

* * *

Some place too much stock in riches. Others despise any form of wealth. We need to learn to place a *proper valuation on wealth*.

> "Better is he who is lightly esteemed and has a servant than he who honors himself and lacks bread" (12:9).

In order to have a servant, one would need to first have a certain degree of wealth. Even though others may have little regard for him, it is better to have this wealth than not. Lacking bread is not honorable (this is different than *sacrificing*, which would be honorable). Therefore, the one who lacks bread will only receive honor from himself. So riches are valuable and should not be quickly disregarded.

> "Better is a little with righteousness than great income with injustice" (16:8).

On the other hand, while riches are valuable, they are not more valuable than righteousness. If the only way to obtain wealth is by dealing unjustly with others, it is better to maintain one's integrity and live in humble circumstances. Righteousness before God will *always* be more important than the riches of this life.

* * *

In developing a proper attitude toward riches, it is important that we understand how our wealth influences others.

> "The poor is hated even by his neighbor, but those who love the rich are many" (14:20).

> "Wealth adds many friends, but a poor man is separated from his friend" (19:4).

A sad reality in life is that many people value friendships based upon what they can get out of the relationship. If someone might be in a position to help them in the form of labor, connections, or material prosperity, many will be more friendly to such a person than to one who is not able to offer such things. This is Solomon's point. People want to be friends with the wealthy in the hopes of obtaining some financial benefit from the relationship. The poor cannot offer this, so they are despised and their friendship is disregarded. Solomon reinforces this point a couple verses after the second one listed above: "Many will seek the favor of a generous man, and every man is a friend to him who gives gifts. All the brothers of a poor man hate him; how much more do his friends abandon him! He pursues them with words, but they are gone" (19:6-7). Sadly, the benefit the poor man has to offer through his *words* (teaching, encouragement, etc.) is not worth nearly as much (in the eyes of many) as the *"gifts"* distributed by the wealthy to his friends.

> "A man's gift makes room for him and brings him before great men" (18:16).

Another sad reality in life is that many are unwilling to help others without getting something in return. For a gift, they will consider helping. Without a gift, and they see no point in even listening. These *gifts* (bribes) are often used to gain favor and special treatment from those in power (*"great men"*).

> *"A gift in secret subdues anger, and a bribe in the bosom, strong wrath"* (21:14).

Just as a gift (bribe) can be used to receive special treatment from those in power, it can also be used to *avoid* harsh treatment from these same officials. When Paul was imprisoned, Felix hoped *"that money would be given him by Paul"* in order to secure his release. When no such bribe was given, he *"left Paul imprisoned"* (Acts 24:26-27). Solomon does not make these statements about bribes in order to suggest that it is *wise* to bribe others in order to gain special treatment. He is simply explaining reality. Our wealth – or lack thereof – has an influence upon others. Bribery is just another example of how this can happen.

Things to Avoid

As we are encouraged to be good stewards of the blessings we have received from God, there are certain things are are to *avoid*.

> *"My son, if you have become surety for your neighbor, have given a pledge for a stranger, if you have been snared with the words of your mouth, have been caught with the words of your mouth, do this then, my son, and deliver yourself; since you*

> *have come into the hand of your neighbor, go, humble yourself, and importune your neighbor. Give no sleep to your eyes, nor slumber to your eyelids; deliver yourself like a gazelle from the hunter's hand and like a bird from the hand of a fowler"* (6:1-5).

This passage is one of a few that makes a very clear warning against becoming the guarantor for someone else's debt. Solomon says that if one has *"become surety"* for another, it is a matter of great urgency that he free himself of that obligation. He says that one ought to go and beg his neighbor to release him of this obligation even before he gets any more sleep. One who has *"become surety"* for another has been *"snared"* and *"caught"* with the words by which he entered into the agreement. He likens this to a gazelle and a bird that is being hunted. There is no benefit for being the guarantor of another's debt, only suffering (11:15). The guarantor will gain nothing, yet risks his own financial and material loss when others are unwilling or unable to pay their own debts (20:16; 27:13; 22:26-27). So Solomon says, *"He who hates being a guarantor is secure"* (11:15). Being a good steward means we will not unnecessarily risk our own livelihood and security through the lack of good stewardship on the part of others.

> *"The rich rules over the poor, and the borrower becomes the lender's slave"* (22:7).

The wise man warns us here against the accumulation of debt. The borrower is under obligation to give a certain amount of the fruits of his labor to the lender. Solomon is not condemning the lender for expecting to be repaid. Rather, he is pointing our the foolishness of entering into a debt obligation unnecessarily. There are times when debt is unavoidable. But the way of the wise is to avoid debt whenever possible and to pay back any debt that exists as quickly as possible, so as to not be under subjection of the entity to which money is owed.

The Application of Wisdom

Justice

Wisdom says, *"I walk in the way of righteousness, in the midst of the paths of justice"* (8:20). Therefore, those who follow after wisdom will learn to appreciate and practice *justice*. In contrast, Solomon says, *"Evil men do not understand justice..."* (28:5). If we wish to be wise, then unlike the evil men, we must *"understand justice."*

Dealing Justly with Others

The most basic and common application of justice is in our dealings with others. Several passages in Proverbs speak to this.

> *"The thoughts of the righteous are just, but the counsels of the wicked are deceitful"* (12:5).

For one to truly deal justly with others requires a sense of justice that is not superficial but that comes from his heart as an integral part of his character. Remember what Solomon says: *"Watch over your heart with all diligence, for from it flow the springs of life"* (4:23). If we are to deal justly with others, our *thoughts* must be just.

> *"The exercise of justice is joy for the righteous, but is terror to the workers of iniquity"* (21:15).

Those who are righteous will rejoice when justice is carried out. In contrast, this same exercising of justice will be a *"terror"* or *"destruction"* (KJV) to those who work iniquity. Why? It is *just* for sin to be punished and for righteousness to be rewarded.

> *"The righteous is concerned for the rights of the poor, the wicked does not understand such concern"* (29:7).

The phrase, *"rights of the poor,"* refers to the application of justice – that the poor will be treated fairly. Often those who are rich are able to manipulate the justice system to their advantage (cf. 17:23). But Solomon is clear: *"To show partiality to the wicked is not good, nor to thrust aside the righteous in judgment"* (18:5; cf. 24:23; 28:21). In order for justice to be carried out, the rich must have no advantage over the poor. However, the poor are not to be given special treatment either, as this is also a perversion of justice. The Law of Moses was clear about this. After telling the people not to *"pervert justice,"* God adds: *"nor shall you be partial to a poor man in his dispute"* (Exodus 23:2-3). For justice to be carried out, *all men* must be treated impartially as equals.

> *"Do not move the ancient boundary which your fathers have set"* (22:28).

> *"Do not move the ancient boundary or go into the fields of the fatherless, for their Redeemer is strong; He will plead their case against you"* (23:10-11).

Brethren have often used the prohibition of moving these ancient landmarks to make the point that we should not try to change what God has revealed to us. This is certainly an important warning. But these passages, rather than containing warnings about our need to hold fast to the instructions which God has revealed to us, are about dealing justly with others. The *"ancient boundary"* would have been a marker to indicate the border of one's property. When one moves these markers, he is essentially *stealing land* from his neighbor. Such stealing was obviously condemned (Exodus 20:15). But the wise man has a specific circumstance in mind in the second passage above: moving the boundaries to take land from *"the fatherless."* These orphans would have no one to stand up for them. It is also likely that they would not even be aware that land was being taken from them. The point then is that we should not take advantage of others, even those who are powerless to stop us or who are unaware of the injustice being done to them.

> *"A false balance is an abomination to the Lord, but a just weight is His delight"* (11:1).

Solomon teaches us here that we are to deal justly in our business transactions. *"Differing weights and differing measures, both of them are abominable to the Lord"* (20:10; cf. 20:23). Why? These differing weights and measures make it possible for one to charge the same price for a lower weight of grain (or whatever else is being sold). As with moving the ancient boundary, it might be possible to use differing weights or a false scale and not get caught by those whom we are cheating. But that does not matter. God knows. Those who cheat others are an abomination to Him. Those who deal justly are His delight.

> *"The first to plead his case seems right, until another comes and examines him. The cast lot puts an end to strife and decides between the mighty ones"* (18:17-18).

The first verse warns us against rushing to judgment before having all the facts and hearing both sides. The *"cast lot"* is a symbol of impartial judgment because the final outcome is unaffected by the will of man. Such impartial judgment is able to end strife and decide between mighty ones. Our exercising of justice must not be based upon human will or partial information but upon an honest examination of all knowable facts in light of the truth.

> *"A wicked man receives a bribe from the bosom to pervert the ways of justice"* (17:23).

At the beginning of this section on *justice*, we noticed this statement by Solomon: *"Evil men do not understand justice"* (28:5). Because they do not understand justice and the value of it, they are willing to receive bribes in order to *"pervert the ways of justice."* Wicked men value material things over that which is right and fair. Those who are righteous will value justice over riches.

> *"A rascally witness makes a mockery of justice, and the mouth of the wicked spreads iniquity"* (19:28).

A *"rascally"* or *"ungodly"* (KJV) witness is one who does not speak the truth, as opposed to a *"trustworthy witness [who] will not lie"* (14:5). A lying witness *"makes a mockery of justice"* because justice is impossible without truth.

> *"The violence of the wicked will drag them away,
> because they refuse to act with justice"* (21:7).

When justice is not carried out, there are negative consequences. Those who commit *violence* (*robbery*, KJV) are dealing unjustly with others. Because they refuse to treat others as they ought to treat them, they will eventually suffer for it themselves, either in this life as their fellow man carries out justice against them or after this life following their appointment at the judgment seat of God.

> *"Abundant food is in the fallow ground of the poor,
> but it is swept away by injustice"* (13:23).

The *"fallow ground"* or *"tillage"* (KJV) of the poor is the land he is able to cultivate to provide for himself. By His providence, God has provided abundant blessings to man that can be obtained by working hard and exercising wisdom. But when one deals unjustly with the poor man by taking away his land or his ability to cultivate it, he is robbing him of the blessings which he might have received by God's providence. If we fail to practice *justice* with our fellow man, we are standing in the way of their receiving divine blessings.

God Will Deal Justly with Us

One reason why it is so important to deal justly with others is because God will deal justly with us.

> *"A just balance and scales belong to the Lord; all the
> weights of the bag are His concern"* (16:11).

God is perfectly fair and impartial. His balance and scales are just. In the King James Version, the second phrase in this verse is translated, *"All the weights of the bag are his work."* The point is that anything that is *fair* and *just* is of God. Therefore, in any dealings He has with man – whether it is in revealing His will or judging us in the end – God will be impartial in judgment.

> *"A false witness will not go unpunished, and he who tells lies will not escape"* (19:5).

Those who are false witnesses are guilty of two offenses. First, and most obviously, they lie. Second, by testifying falsely about or against others, they are preventing others from receiving just treatment from men (cf. 19:28). It is no wonder then that God would punish those who offer false testimony.

> *"The poor man and the oppressor have this in common: the Lord gives light to the eyes of both"* (29:13).

Both men – the poor man and the one who oppresses him – are subject to divine judgment. The phrase, *"the Lord gives light to the eyes of both,"* means that God provides life and the ability to understand truth (and with understanding *truth* comes an understanding of *justice*) to both men. The oppressor has no excuse for treating others in the way that he does. God, as his Maker, will hold him accountable.

The Application of Wisdom

Suffering

Suffering is a reality of life. Job said, *"Man, who is born of woman, is short-lived and full of turmoil"* (Job 14:1). Job certainly experienced more trouble in life than most do, but suffering exists for us all. The book of Proverbs contains instructions that will help us deal with the troubles of this life.

Dealing with Our Own Suffering

The first person's suffering we have to learn how to deal with is our own. In order to do this, we need to understand the realities and challenges we face during hard times.

> *"Hope deferred makes the heart sick, but desire fulfilled is a tree of life"* (13:12).

It is natural for disappointing circumstances to affect us. When events in life occur as we would hope, the wise man describes this as *"a tree of life."* Yet when hope is *deferred*, meaning that which we desire is left unfulfilled, it has a negative impact upon us. Dealing with suffering does not mean we ignore the reality of it or deny that it can be a challenge. To do so only sets us up to be overcome by it.

> *"The heart knows its own bitterness, and a stranger does not share its joy"* (14:10).

In making a point about divine revelation, Paul expressed a fundamental truth about the thoughts of man: *"For who among men knows the thoughts of man except the spirit of the man which is in him?"* (1 Corinthians 2:11). Each person is well-acquainted with the sorrows he experiences in life. Strangers do not have the insight into one's thoughts that he does. So while others may try to help when one is suffering, such help may not always seem adequate. This is not because those who try to help are not as concerned as they ought to be. It is simply because it is impossible for them to know the thoughts, circumstances, and experiences of the sufferer as he does.

> *"A joyful heart makes a cheerful face, but when the heart is sad, the spirit is broken"* (15:13).

Suffering within one's heart will often affect how one presents himself before others. Though there are times when one may try to hide his sorrow (cf. 14:13), generally one indicates through facial expressions and body language the mood of his heart. Hence, the *"joyful heart makes a cheerful face."* However, Solomon tells us that *"when the heart is sad, the spirit is broken."* Sorrow, particularly excessive and prolonged sorrow, makes it difficult for one's spiritual life to be healthy. If we allow the hardships and calamities of this life to cause us to forget the great blessings and promises of God, then we pass from a state of difficulty into utter despair.

> *"All the days of the afflicted are bad, but a cheerful heart has a continual feast"* (15:15).

The wise man contrasts one who is *"afflicted"* with one who has *"a cheerful heart."* The implication is that the one who is *"afflicted"* is not just one who faces difficult circumstances (which we all do), but it refers to one whose attitude is such that he has reached the point in which his *"spirit is broken"* (15:13). For such a person with no positive outlook or hope, every day will be bad. But the one with a *"cheerful heart,"* though he may experience troubles in life, is able to have a *"continual feast"* as he recognizes the blessings he has that come from above.

> *"A joyful heart is good medicine, but a broken spirit dries up the bones"* (17:22).

This verse mentions the importance of having a positive outlook. The *"broken spirit"* that has forgotten the goodness that God shows to us *"dries up the bones."* Later, Solomon asks, *"The spirit of a man can endure his sickness, but as for a broken spirit who can bear it?"* (18:14). In contrast, having a *"joyful heart"* does us good. This is not describing the heart of one who ignores the problems of life and allows himself to hold onto a false hope. Rather, the one with a *"joyful heart"* is one who recognizes the good with which God has blessed him and the promises for the faithful despite his circumstances.

Dealing with the Suffering of Others

We can all see that *suffering* is a reality in our own lives. But we must recognize that others face troubles in life as well. We cannot focus only on ourselves. We should try to help others when they are hurting. But we must be careful that we offer the right kind of help; otherwise, we may only make their suffering worse.

> *"Even in laughter the heart may be in pain, and the end of joy may be grief"* (14:13).

It is possible for one to be suffering, but we are unaware of it because they have tried to cover it up behind a facade of laughter and joy. This is a reminder for us that we should not be too quick to dismiss the possibility that one may need our encouragement, support, or sympathy even though they try to put on a cheerful face when they are going through hardships.

> *"Like one who takes off a garment on a cold day, or like vinegar on soda, is he who sings songs to a troubled heart"* (25:20).

Solomon's point in this verse is simply that some things are not appropriate in certain situations. There may be a time to remove a coat, but it is not on a cold day. Mixing vinegar and soda together causes a reaction, rending the soda (*nitre*, KJV) useless. There is a time to sing songs, particularly in a time of joy (cf. James 5:13). But such careless cheerfulness is not appropriate – and is often unwelcome – when one is going through a time of grief. We must do our best to be aware of the feelings and hardships of others so that we do not act in an inappropriate manner, thus causing further grief to their already *"troubled heart."*

The Application of Wisdom

Alcohol

Despite the warnings in the book of Proverbs and the rest of the Scriptures against both the destructive and casual uses of alcohol, many claim that a Christian is free to drink alcohol, just so long as he does not become *drunk*. In light of this, it is especially important to note what the book of Proverbs has to say about *alcohol*.

> *"Wine is a mocker, strong drink a brawler, and whoever is intoxicated by it is not wise"* (20:1).

Solomon begins this verse by saying, *"Wine is a mocker."* Alcohol has the ability to make a fool out of someone. It allows one to *think* he is in control when he really is not. The point is made later in the book that alcohol alters the way one thinks (31:5). It is a *"mocker"* to those who believe they can partake in the consumption of alcohol without being affected by it. Next, the wise man says, *"Strong drink* [is] *a brawler."* This refers to the violent tendencies of one who is given to alcohol and how it causes trouble for both the drinker and those around him. So Solomon says, *"Whoever is intoxicated by it is not wise."* We have been studying how to *apply* wisdom. If we are to follow the wisdom that comes from above, we must avoid the sin of *drunkenness*.

> *"Do not be with heavy drinkers of wine, or with gluttonous eaters of meat; for the heavy drinker and*

> the glutton will come to poverty, and drowsiness will clothe one with rags" (23:20-21).

Solomon groups the sins of drunkenness and gluttony together in these verses. He warns that we should not be *"with"* them, meaning that we should not go along with them so that we put ourselves in a position to be tempted to practice their sins. We cannot avoid all contact with sinful people (cf. 1 Corinthians 5:9-10); but we can avoid putting ourselves in situations in which we will be tempted to give into *peer pressure* and do what others are doing. Furthermore, Solomon makes a point here about *stewardship*. He warns that the *"heavy drinker...will come to poverty."* Not only is such use of alcohol to be avoided because it has a negative effect upon one's thinking, but also because it is a waste of money.

Solomon's Warning About Alcohol

> "Who has woe? Who has sorrow? Who has contentions? Who has complaining? Who has wounds without cause? Who has redness of eyes? Those who linger long over wine, those who go to taste mixed wine.
>
> "Do not look at the wine when it is red, when it sparkles in the cup, when it goes down smoothly; at the last it bites like a serpent and stings like a viper.
>
> "Your eyes will see strange things and your mind will utter perverse things. And you will be like one who lies down in the middle of the sea, or like one who lies down on the top of a mast. 'They struck me, but I did not become ill; they beat me, but I did not

know it. When shall I awake? I will seek another drink'" (23:29-35).

The above passage contains clear warning from Solomon about the dangers of alcohol. Many will try to justify the casual use of alcohol (often referred to as *"social drinking"*); but given how destructive alcohol can be, Solomon warns that one should not even go this far.

"Who has woe... sorrow... contentions... complaining... wounds without cause... redness of eyes? Those who linger long over wine, those who go to taste mixed wine" (23:29-30). Though people often resort to alcohol in an attempt to *escape* their problems (cf. 31:6-7), Solomon warns that trouble comes to those who *"linger long over wine"* (implying *drunkenness*) and those who *"seek* [KJV] *mixed wine"* (implying the pursuit of alcohol, which would necessarily be *before* drunkenness). The problems caused by alcohol affect every aspect of one's life – emotionally (*"woe"* suggests the idea of *lamentation*); financially (*"sorrow"* is from a word suggesting *want*, in the sense that one comes to be *in need*); socially (*"contentions"* denote the strife and discord that will exist between the drinker and others); verbally (*"complaining"* or *"babbling"* [KJV] refers to the fact that one will not be able to communicate effectively); mentally (*"wounds without cause"* are those wounds one suffers that he cannot recall how he received them because his memory has been affected by the alcohol); and physically (*"redness of eyes"*). Alcohol is not something to be treated lightly.

"Do not look on the wine when it is red, when it sparkles in the cup, when it goes down smoothly; at the last it bites like a serpent and stings like a viper" (23:31-32). Those who believe that the casual use of alcohol (*"social drinking"*) is acceptable, just so long as one does not proceed to *drunkenness*, need to remember this verse. Rather than advising one to enjoy alcohol in moderation, Solomon warns that one should not even look at it! Though it may *go down smoothly*, it will cause trouble for the one who consumes it. Far from condoning the drinking of alcohol in moderation, Solomon instead warns that one should not even look at it, lest he be tempted to take the first drink.

"Your eyes will see strange things and your mind will utter perverse things" (23:33). Alcohol affects one's perception of reality so that he sees *"strange things."* It also loosens one's tongue so that – rather than filtering out speech that would be improper, offensive, contentious, and unwise – one who consumes alcohol will be more inclined to say those things which should not be said.

"And you will be like one who lies down in the middle of the sea, or like one who lies down on the top of a mast. 'They struck me, but I did not become ill; they beat me, but I did not know it'" (23:34-35). Alcohol makes one oblivious to his surroundings (as *"one who lies down in the middle of the sea"*) and unaware of any danger in which he may be (as *"one who lies down on the top of a mast"*). Furthermore, alcohol dulls pain (*"they beat me, but I did not know it"*) so that the natural reflex to recoil from pain and flee from harm is absent, thus putting the drinker in the position to be harmed even further.

"'When shall I awake? I will seek another drink'" (23:35). This phrase reminds us of the addictive nature of alcohol. Despite all the trouble that comes to those who are given to it, many will continue to go back to it.

Warning to Lemuel About Alcohol

> *"It is not for kings, O Lemuel, it is not for kings to drink wine, or for rulers to desire strong drink, for they will drink and forget what is decreed, and pervert the rights of all the afflicted.*
>
> *"Give strong drink to him who is perishing, and wine to him whose life is bitter. Let him drink and forget his poverty and remember his trouble no more"* (31:4-7).

This passage is sometimes used by those who want to condone the use of alcohol as a means of dealing with one's problems. Many claim to use alcohol as a way to handle the stress they have from their home, work, or love lives. Yet if we consider the context, there is another point altogether that we should take from this passage.

"It is not for kings, O Lemuel, it is not for kings to drink wine, or for rulers to desire strong drink, for they will drink and forget what is decreed, and pervert the rights of all the afflicted" **(31:4-5).** First of all, we should note that this instruction is directed toward *kings*. There is a reason behind this. Because a king is in a position of authority over others, there is much more harm that can come from his use of alcohol than others. This passage mentions two reasons why kings and rulers are to avoid alcohol. First, *"they will drink and forget what is decreed"* (31:5). When they forget the difference between right and wrong, it becomes impossible for them to rule effectively or fairly. Second, they will *"pervert the rights of all the afflicted"* (31:5). This does harm to others because it denies them the *justice* that they deserve. So the admonition is for kings and rulers not to *"drink"* or even *"desire"* alcohol (31:4). The instruction to not *"desire"* it means that the use of alcohol should never even reach the point of *casual* use (*"social drinking"*), let alone the *destructive* use (*drunkenness*).

"Give strong drink to him who is perishing, and wine to him whose life is bitter. Let him drink and forget his poverty and remember his trouble no more" **(31:6-7).** These verses are seen by some as an authorization for the use of alcohol as a way for one to deal with the hardships of life. Yet this does not fit at all with the other passages in Proverbs that identify alcohol as the *cause* of so many hardships in life (23:20-21, 29-35). And while the Bible does authorize the *medicinal* use of alcohol for physical ailments (1 Timothy 5:23), this passage is talking about mental and emotional hardships. The alcohol, because it alters one's thinking, thus allowing him to *"forget his poverty and remember his trouble no more"* (31:7), is appealing to many. But instead of *authorizing* the practice, this passage simply mentions it as a *common* practice. A practice being *common* certainly does not make it right. The context emphasizes *sober-mindedness* (31:5). One who is to be *sober-minded* – such as the king of this context – must ignore what others are doing, leave them to their devices, and avoid alcohol himself so that he can do what he is responsible to do. Rather than condoning the use of alcohol as a way to forget the troubles of life, this passage teaches us that we must *avoid* alcohol so that we can think clearly and do those things which God would have us to do.

The Application of Wisdom

Plans for the Future

Some Christians spend little time thinking about and planning for the future because, in their minds, God is in control so the future is of no concern to them. Certainly, God is in control. Yet this does not mean that we have no responsibility to plan for the future. The book of Proverbs contains instructions that admonish us to prepare for the future, yet still acknowledge God in all things.

> *"The plans of the heart belong to man, but the answer of the tongue is from the Lord"* (16:1).

> *"The mind of man plans his way, but the Lord directs his steps"* (16:9).

We are responsible for decisions and plans we have to make in life. Yet we are not to forget our responsibility before God. Though in our minds we may plan our way, we must allow the Lord, through His word, to direct our steps. The wise man says in this same chapter: *"Commit your works to the Lord and your plans will be established"* (16:3). Our primary obligation is to faithfully obey God. Therefore, any plans we make must revolve around that responsibility.

> *"The horse is prepared for the day of battle, but victory belongs to the Lord"* (21:31).

There is a tendency for man to place a great deal of faith in himself and his resources, especially in the realm of military affairs. The prophet Isaiah warned about this: *"Woe to those who go down to Egypt for help and rely on horses, and trust in chariots because they are many and in horsemen because they are very strong, but they do not look to the Holy One of Israel, nor seek the Lord!"* (Isaiah 31:1). Solomon says, *"Victory belongs to the Lord,"* implying that without God, victory will not be possible. However, this does not mean that our plans and preparations are futile. The horse that is *"prepared for the day of battle"* must still be prepared, or else defeat will be certain. The point is that we must do what we are able to do (make whatever preparations we can make for the future) and put our trust in God for all those things which are out of our control.

> *"Do not boast about tomorrow, for you do not know what a day may bring forth"* (27:1).

James wrote something very similar to this in his epistle, warning those who were making plans for the future not to *"boast"* because they did *"not know what* [their lives] *will be like tomorrow."* He added: *"Instead, you ought to say, 'If the Lord wills, we will live and also do this or that'"* (James 4:13-16). The making of plans for the future is not condemned by Solomon, nor was it condemned by James. Instead, this is a warning against the arrogant mindset in which one believes that the uncertainties of the future will have no effect on him.

> *"Surely there is a future, and your hope will not be cut off"* (23:18).

While many things in the future are uncertain and out of our control, we should not despair. The people of God have something to which they can look forward, even if it is not necessarily in this life. Though the book of Proverbs emphasizes the fact that there are often temporal blessings of life that come when we follow after wisdom, these are *general* and not *absolute* statements. Regardless of what blessings come or do not come in this life as a result of our following the wisdom that comes from above, God offers to the faithful *"a future"* and *"hope"* beyond this life. So the apostle Paul encouraged the brethren in Colossae: *"Set your mind on the things above, not on the things that are on earth"* (Colossians 3:2). To the brethren in Corinth he wrote: *"For we know that if the earthly tent which is our house is torn down, we have a building from God, a house not made with hands, eternal in the heavens"* (2 Corinthians 5:1). Peter wrote of our *"living hope through the resurrection of Jesus Christ from the dead, to obtain an inheritance which is imperishable and undefiled and will not fade away, reserved in heaven for you"* (1 Peter 1:3-4). Though the book of Proverbs focuses much on this life, we must not lose sight of the eternal hope that the people of God have through Christ.

The Application of Wisdom

Women

Since much of the book of Proverbs is directed toward the wise man's son, Solomon spends a lot of time discussing *women*. He warns his son about certain women who are to be avoided. He also gives instruction about the blessings of a good wife and discusses her character so that she might be identified.

Warnings About the Adulteress

Though much of the book of Proverbs contains brief instructions on a broad range of topics, there are several lengthy sections dealing with the dangers of the adulteress. This alone should serve as a warning to us about the severe threat that immoral women pose to godly men. So the wise man earnestly pleads with his son to not follow after the adulteress.

> *"My son, give attention to my wisdom, incline your ear to my understanding; that you may observe discretion and your lips may reserve knowledge. For the lips of an adulteress drip honey and smoother than oil is her speech; but in the end she is bitter as wormwood, sharp as a two-edged sword. Her feet go down to death, her steps take hold of Sheol. She does not ponder the path of life; her ways are unstable, she does not know it.*

> *"Now then, my sons, listen to me and do not depart from the words of my mouth. Keep your way far from her and do not go near the door of her house, or you will give your vigor to others and your years to the cruel one; and strangers will be filled with your strength and your hard-earned goods will go to the house of an alien; and you groan at your final end, when your flesh and your body are consumed; and you say, 'How I have hated instruction! And my heart spurned reproof! I have not listened to the voice of my teachers, nor inclined my ear to my instructors! I was almost in utter ruin in the midst of the assembly and congregation"* (5:1-14).

"My son, give attention to my wisdom..." (5:1-2). Solomon begins this section with yet another call for his son to *hear* instruction. These warnings are worthless if one does not pay attention to them.

"For the lips of an adulteress drip honey and smoother than oil is her speech; but in the end she is bitter as wormwood, sharp as a two-edged sword" (5:3-4). The first way Solomon mentions in which the adulteress tempts men is through her *words*. Through her speech, she makes herself appealing and available. This is discussed further in a later passage (7:13-21). However, anything can seem good and appealing if we ignore the consequences. Though the adulteress uses words to make both herself and the act of fornication seem attractive, the end result is *"bitter as wormwood."* As Solomon says later: *"The mouth of an adulteress is a deep pit; he who is cursed of the Lord will fall into it"* (22:14).

***"Her feet go down to death, her steps take hold of Sheol"* (5:5).** Because of her sinful ways, she is headed toward destruction. Those who follow after her will find themselves with the same fate (cf. 7:26-27).

***"She does not ponder the path of life; her ways are unstable, she does not know it"* (5:6).** The New American Standard translates this as though *the adulteress* does not *"ponder the path of life."* However, the King James Version reads: *"Lest thou shouldest ponder the path of life,"* implying that the young man being warned by his father should not forget to *"ponder the path of life."* In either case, the point for the young man to whom this is written is that he should consider the adulteress and the instability of her ways and not follow after her.

***"Now then, my sons, listen to me and do not depart from the words of my mouth. Keep your way far from her and do not go near the door of her house"* (5:7-8).** Though Solomon began this section addressing his *"son"* (5:1), he now addresses *"my sons"* (5:7), implying that this instruction was not just for one particular person in a unique set of circumstances. The problem he addresses is common enough that all can learn from his instruction here. So he warns the young men to keep *"far from her and do not go near the door of her house"* (5:8). It is foolish for one to put himself in a difficult situation unnecessarily. If temptation can be avoided by keeping far away from the temptress, then this ought to be done. One should not see how close he can get to sin or temptation. As much as is in his power, he should stay far away from it.

"Or you will give your vigor to others and your years to the cruel one; and strangers will be filled with your strength

and your hard-earned goods will go to the house of an alien; and you will groan at your final end, when your flesh and your body are consumed" **(5:9-11).** In these verses, Solomon mentions three ways in which the adulteress causes harm to those who go after her. First, there are *personal* consequences (5:9) as one gives away his *"vigor"* or *"honour"* (KJV). The point is that one's reputation is ruined by his association with the adulteress. His years will go *"to the cruel one"* because of the future hardships he will have to endure because of his choices. Second, there are *financial* consequences (5:10) as *"strangers will be filled with* [his] *strength and* [his] *hard-earned goods will go to the house of an alien"* (cf. 6:26; 29:3). Third, there are *physical* consequences (5:11) as his *"flesh and…body are consumed,"* referring to the negative effects and disease that are often associated with sexual promiscuity. Though sexual sin often seems appealing at the beginning, Solomon affirms that one who follows after the adulteress *"will groan at* [his] *final end."*

"And you say, 'How I have hated instruction! And my heart spurned reproof! I have not listened to the voice of my teachers, nor inclined my ear to my instructors! I was almost in utter ruin in the midst of the assembly and congregation'" (5:12-14). One who follows after the adulteress will have to live with the guilt and regret of his sin. Solomon points out that it is not for lack of instruction that one falls prey to the temptress. Wise counsel will always advise one to avoid the adulteress. So for one to engage in this sin, he must *hate* instruction, *spurn* reproof, and *not listen* to those who try to guide him in the paths of wisdom. Once he comes to his senses, he will have to deal with the consequences of his sin, the guilt associated with his actions, and the mental anguish of knowing that all of this could have been completely avoided if he had just listened to his counselors. We would do well to learn from instructions like this, rather than having to make the same mistakes ourselves.

* * *

> *"...to keep you from the evil woman, from the smooth tongue of the adulteress.*
>
> *"Do not desire her beauty in your heart, nor let her capture you with her eyelids. For on account of a harlot one is reduced to a loaf of bread, and an adulteress hunts precious life.*
>
> *"Can a man take fire in his bosom and his clothes not be burned? Or can a man walk on hot coals and his feet not be scorched? So is the one who goes in to his neighbor's wife; whoever touches her will not go unpunished. Men do not despise a thief if he steals to satisfy himself when he is hungry; but when he is found, he must repay sevenfold; he must give all the substance of his house. The one who commits adultery with a woman is lacking sense; he who would destroy himself does it. Wounds and disgrace he will find, and his reproach will not be blotted out. For jealousy enrages a man, and he will not spare in the day of vengeance. He will not accept any ransom, nor will he be satisfied though you give many gifts"* (6:24-35).

"To keep you from the evil woman, from the smooth tongue of the adulteress" (6:24). Prior to this verse, Solomon has issued another call for his son to *"observe the commandment* of your father and...the teaching of your mother" (6:20). This instruction is designed to *"keep* [one] *from the evil woman."*

"Do not desire her beauty in your heart, nor let her capture you with her eyelids" (6:25). The first thing that one would notice about this woman is the way that she looks. No transgression is committed by merely *seeing* a woman. Instead, Solomon warns: *"Lust not after her beauty in thine heart"* (KJV). Jesus later warned: *"Everyone who looks at a woman with lust for her has already committed adultery with her in his heart"* (Matthew 5:28). When one lusts after a woman, thereby committing adultery with her in his heart, it makes it that much easier to commit the actual act of adultery when the opportunity presents itself. So the wise man warns that one should not focus on the adulteress and lust after her. He then warns about one receiving the attention of the adulteress (*"nor let her capture you with her eyelids"*). With a look she is able to capture the attention of her victim and extend an implicit invitation for him to act upon the lust that is in his heart.

"For on account of a harlot one is reduced to a loaf of bread, and an adulteress hunts for the precious life" (6:26). One being *"reduced to a loaf of bread"* refers to the financial hardship that comes to one who goes after the adulteress, as he is unable to afford other food. Other passages also warn about this (5:10; 29:3). But Solomon also warns here that the *"adulteress hunts for the precious life."* She is actively trying to find someone to seduce, rather than being caught herself, unwittingly, in a compromising situation.

"Can a man take fire in his bosom and his clothes not be burned? Or can a man walk on hot coals and his feet not be scorched? So is the one who goes in to his neighbor's wife;

whoever touches her will not go unpunished" **(6:27-29).** Some take Solomon's analogy of one taking *"fire in his bosom"* and apply it to one *lusting* after a woman. Lust is certainly condemned in this context (6:25), but this verse is making a different point. Taking fire in one's bosom and walking on hot coals are not referring to *lust*, but to the actual *act of adultery* (*"the one who goes in to his neighbor's wife"*). Solomon's point is that committing adultery produces some unavoidable and destructive consequences.

"Men do not despise a thief if he steals to satisfy himself when he is hungry; but when he is found, he must repay sevenfold; he must give all the substance of his house" **(6:30-31).** These verses are not condoning theft under certain circumstances (hunger). Rather, Solomon points out that although theft is always wrong, man is often sympathetic toward one who steals solely for the purpose of feeding himself or his family. But even though one might be sympathetic, the thief must still make restitution for his crime.

"The one who commits adultery with a woman is lacking sense; he who would destroy himself does it" **(6:32).** Contrary to the thief stealing in order to feed himself who might find sympathy on account of his circumstances, *"the one who commits adultery...is lacking sense."* There is no excuse for this and it only leads to trouble. This is explained further in the following verses.

"Wounds and disgrace he will find, and his reproach will not be blotted out. For jealousy enrages a man, and he will not spare in the day of vengeance. He will not accept any ransom, nor will he be satisfied though you give many gifts" **(6:33-35).** Though one may be willing to forgive a hungry thief who

makes restitution, there will be no such forgiveness for the adulterer. The rage of a jealous husband will be directed without mercy toward the one who gave in to the temptress. No ransom can be paid that will make restitution for what has been done. There will be no excuses that could ever justify one's actions. Instead, the one who follows after the adulteress will have to suffer *wounds* (threats of physical harm, or actual physical harm, against him from the husband who was wronged by him), *disgrace* (his reputation will be ruined), and *reproach* that will not be blotted out (people will continue to remember and hold a grudge against him for what he has done).

*　*　**

> *"My son, keep my words and treasure my commandments within you. Keep my commandments and live, and my teaching as the apple of your eye. Bind them on your fingers; write them on the tablet of your heart. Say to wisdom, 'You are my sister,' and call understanding your intimate friend; that they may keep you from an adulteress, from the foreigner who flatters with her words.*
>
> *"For at the window of my house I looked out through my lattice, and I saw among the naive, and discerned among the youths a young man lacking sense, passing through the street near her corner; and he takes the way to her house, in the twilight, in the evening, in the middle of the night and in the darkness. And behold, a woman comes out to meet him, dressed as a harlot and cunning of heart. She is*

boisterous and rebellious, her feet do not remain at home; she is now in the streets, now in the squares, and lurks by every corner.

"So she seizes him and kisses him and with a brazen face she says to him: 'I was due to offer peace offerings; today I have paid my vows. Therefore I have come out to meet you, to seek your presence earnestly, and I have found you. I have spread my couch with coverings, with colored linens of Egypt. I have sprinkled my bed with myrrh, aloes and cinnamon. Come, let us drink our fill of love until morning; let us delight ourselves with caresses. For my husband is not at home, he has gone on a long journey; he has taken a bag of money with him, at the full moon he will come home.' With many persuasions she entices him; with her flattering lips she seduces him. Suddenly he follows her as an ox goes to the slaughter, or as one in fetters to the discipline of a fool, until an arrow pierces through his liver; as a bird hastens to the snare, so he does not know that it will cost him his life.

"Now therefore, my sons, listen to me, and pay attention to the words of my mouth. Do not let your heart turn aside to her ways, do not stray into her paths. For many are the victims she has cast down, and numerous are all her slain. Her house is the way to Sheol, descending to the chambers of death" (7:1-27).

"My son, keep my words and treasure my commandments within you. [...] That they may keep you from an adulteress,

from the foreigner who flatters with her words" **(7:1-5).** Yet again, we have a father issuing a warning to his son about the dangers of the adulteress (cf. 5:1-2; 6:20-24). Certain instructions are often repeated for emphasis. This is certainly a topic that the wise man wants to impress upon his son.

"For at the window of my house I looked out through my lattice, and I saw among the naive, and discerned among the youths a young man lacking sense" **(7:6-7).** The dangers that one may allow himself to experience in his naivete are often observable to others. The wise man talks about being able to see how a young man is getting himself dangerously close to temptation. Yet the young man is oblivious to the trouble that is coming because he is *"lacking sense."* In other words, he has closed his mind to wisdom and is foolishly putting himself in a position to be severely tempted. We need to have enough sense and awareness to avoid temptation whenever possible.

"Passing through the street near her corner; and he takes the way to her house, in the twilight, in the evening, in the middle of the night and in the darkness" **(7:8-9).** This young man foolishly puts himself in a dangerous situation. He finds himself in the wrong place (*"near her corner;* [on] *the way to her house"*) at the wrong time (*"in the twilight…evening…middle of the night…darkness"*), not by chance, but by choice.

"And behold, a woman comes to meet him, dressed as a harlot and cunning of heart" **(7:10).** We have already noticed how the adulteress is *actively* trying to capture one in sin – *"An adulteress hunts for the precious life"* (6:26). Here, after the naive young man foolishly takes the way past her house, she seizes the opportunity and goes out to meet him. The first thing he will notice about this woman is her clothing. She wears *"the* *attire of an harlot"* (KJV), which will only add fuel to the fire of any lustful thoughts he may have. This is deliberate on her part, as she is *"cunning of heart."* But what any woman ought to remember is that if she goes out *"dressed as a harlot,"* wearing clothing that *invites* lust, she has complicity in the sin of one who lusts after her, regardless of whether or not her intention was to seduce him (as was the intention of the harlot).

***"She is boisterous and rebellious, her feet do not remain at home; she is now in the streets, now in the squares, and lurks by every corner"* (7:11-12).** This woman is the opposite of the quiet and submissive wife that was later commended by the apostle Paul (1 Timothy 2:11). The adulteress is *"boisterous and rebellious"* instead. Solomon says, *"Her feet do not remain at home"* because she is uninterested in the domestic role which God gave to women (Genesis 2:18; Titus 2:4-5).

***"So she seizes him and kisses him and with a brazen face she says to him: 'I was due to offer peace offerings; today I have paid my vows. Therefore I have come out to meet you, to seek your presence earnestly, and I have found you. I have spread my couch with coverings, with colored linens of Egypt. I have sprinkled my bed with myrrh, aloes and cinnamon'"* (7:13-17).** Solomon warns that the adulteress will do everything she can do to make the act of adultery *convenient*. Already she has been described as coming out to the young man, rather than waiting for him to come to her (7:10). She dresses as a harlot in order to incite lust in his heart (7:10). She is wild and rebellious, suggesting that she is interested in fulfilling any worldly and sensual desire she may have, rather than submitting to the will of God (7:11). She is already out in the streets and the squares (7:11-12). Then in these verses, she initiates the affair when she *"seizes him and kisses him"* (7:13). Her statement about peace offerings suggests that, in her mind, she has fulfilled any religious obligation she may have had, thus freeing her time now to do as she pleases (7:14). She makes this young man feel wanted by stating that she has sought him earnestly, while also implying that she is ready for the affair without any persuasions from him (7:15). She has even prepared the place for their sexual encounter ahead of time (7:16-17). She has done whatever she can to remove any roadblock that might delay the affair, reducing the time he might have to realize the terrible mistake he is about to make and flee from her.

***"'Come, let us drink our fill of love until morning; let us delight ourselves with caresses'"* (7:18).** Her offer is appealing to many – to satisfy sexual desires without any long-term commitment. Her invitation is just *"until morning."* It is all about fulfilling one's *desire* without any sense of *responsibility*.

***"'For my husband is not at home, he has gone on a long journey; he has taken a bag of money with him, at the full moon he will come home'"* (7:19-20).** One of the dangers of committing adultery with another man's wife is having to later deal with her jealous husband [see comments on 6:33-35]. Yet she convinces the young man that no one will catch them – not even her husband as he has *"gone on a long journey"* and will not be home anytime soon. Of course, even if one's fellow man does not find out, God still knows (cf. Genesis 39:7-10). But in the heat of the moment, one who is being tempted often forgets God. So the promise of not being caught by man becomes very enticing.

"With her many persuasions she entices him; with her flattering lips she seduces him. Suddenly he follows her as an ox goes to the slaughter, or as one in fetters to the discipline of a fool, until an arrow pierces through his liver; as a bird hastens to the snare, so he does not know that it will cost him his life" **(7:21-23).** After all that she does to seduce him, *"Suddenly he follows her"* (7:22). *Suddenly* his will-power gives way to the lust of his heart. Solomon makes no specific mention of the affair after the young man decides to engage in it. It is implied, of course. But it is significant that the time in which they would *"drink* [their] *fill of love until morning"* on her bed *"sprinkled...with myrrh, aloes and cinnamon"* (7:17-18) is completely skipped over in the text. Instead, Solomon goes straight to the consequences of these actions – slaughter, discipline, and a snare. Once sin has been committed and the negative consequences start to take effect, the *"passing pleasures of sin"* (Hebrews 11:25) are suddenly no longer worth mentioning.

"Now therefore, my sons, listen to me, and pay attention to the words of my mouth. Do not let your heart turn aside to her ways, do not stray into her paths. For many are the victims she has cast down, and numerous are all her slain. Her house is the way of Sheol, descending to the chambers of death" **(7:24-27).** The harlot can make adultery convenient, enticing, and seemingly without consequences. But there is no escaping God's judgment. Many have become victims to her. The end result of their sin is death.

* * *

"The woman of folly is boisterous, she is naive and knows nothing. She sits at the doorway of her house,

> *on a seat by the high places of the city, calling to those who pass by, who are making their paths straight: 'Whoever is naive, let him turn in here,' and to him who lacks understanding she says, 'Stolen water is sweet; and bread eaten in secret is pleasant.' But he does not know that the dead are there, that her guests are in the depths of Sheol"* (9:13-18).

"The woman of folly is boisterous, she is naive and knows nothing" (9:13). The *"woman of folly"* here is the adulteress who has been discussed previously. Solomon points out again that she is *"boisterous,"* rather than possessing the quiet spirit that women ought to have [see comments on 7:11]. She is also *"naive,"* proving by her actions that she knows nothing of God's wisdom – or if she does know of it, she at least does not understand the importance of it since she is rejecting it – nor of the consequences that will come upon her for her actions.

"She sits at the doorway of her house, on a seat by the high places of the city, calling to those who pass by, who are making their paths straight: 'Whoever is naive, let him turn in here'" (9:14-16). Earlier in this chapter, Wisdom offers the same invitation as the adulteress: *"Whoever is naive, let him turn in here!"* (9:4; cf. 1:22-23; 8:5-6). One of the reasons why the book of Proverbs is written is *"to give prudence to the naive"* (1:4). Such prudence will lead one away from the adulteress. So she must make her appeal to these same naive persons so that she might catch them *before* they acquire the wisdom that comes from above. Yet she also addresses those *"who are making their paths straight"* (9:15). One may be following the path of righteousness and still give in to the temptress. But in order for this to happen, he must forget the words of wisdom and the consequences for wickedness. Sadly, this happens all too often. Therefore, even those who are walking straight must guard themselves from the temptations of the adulteress, lest he forgets the severity of her sin and, eventually, follows her into sin.

"And to him who lacks understanding she says, 'Stolen water is sweet; and bread eaten in secret is pleasant'" **(9:16-17).** Besides the pleasure that one might normally experience from sexual relations, the adulteress tries to make the affair with her seem even more appealing than legitimate sexual relations. She does this by claiming that those things which are *stolen* and *secret* are *sweet* and *pleasant*. Many desire the excitement that comes from being involved in a forbidden affair, so the adulteress makes this appeal. Yet all of this ignores the consequences that Solomon points out in the next verse.

"But he does not know that the dead are there, that her guests are in the depths of Sheol" **(9:18).** Every appeal of the adulteress is meant to focus on temporary pleasures. She ignores everything that pertains to the future – particularly man's eternal fate after this life. But Solomon ends with this sober reminder: those who give in to the temptations of the adulteress will only have death and destruction to which they can look forward.

* * *

"For a harlot is a deep pit and an adulterous woman is a narrow well. Surely she lurks as a robber, and increases the faithless among men" (23:27-28).

As Solomon has already pointed out, the adulteress is a *trap* who ensnares men (6:26). She convinces them to reject the invitation offered by divine wisdom (9:4) in favor of the temporary pleasures which she offers (9:16-17).

> *"This is the way of an adulteress woman: she eats and wipes her mouth, and says, 'I have done no wrong'"* (30:20).

This woman has departed so far from the will of God that she feels no remorse for her actions. She has become callous in her conscience and believes that she is not doing anything wrong.

> *"A man who loves wisdom makes his father glad, but he who keeps company with harlots wastes his wealth"* (29:3).

Besides the more obvious consequences of adultery, Solomon reminds us again of the fact that association with harlots causes one to squander his money (cf. 5:10; 6:26). So aside from sexual immorality, one who follows after the adulteress is also guilty of failing to exercise good stewardship over the blessings he has received from God.

* * *

After considering the warnings about the adulteress, we turn our attention to the *excellent wife* who is commended to us in the book of Proverbs. There are two basic points that are addressed: the *blessings* and the *character* of the excellent wife.

The Blessings of a Good Wife

Though the adulteress promises the temporary fulfillment of sexual desires without any long-term commitment (7:18), the wise man makes it clear that it is far better to seek after a good wife than to follow after the adulteress.

> *"An excellent wife is the crown of her husband, but she who shames him is like rottenness to his bones"* (12:4).

A few of the passages in the book of Proverbs that discuss the blessings of the good wife make a contrast between her and the one who causes trouble for her husband. It is important to note that Solomon is not encouraging his son to marry simply for the sake of getting married. A wife who *"shames"* her husband *"is like rottenness to his bones."* There are some women who – because of their godless, contentious, and self-absorbed character – are not worthy of consideration when one is looking for a spouse. But an *"excellent wife"* – if one is patient enough to find her – *"is the crown of her husband."*

> *"He who finds a wife finds a good thing and obtains favor from the Lord"* (18:22).

Remembering what Solomon says in the verse previously considered (12:4), the wife being discussed in this verse is not just any wife but is the *excellent* wife. In the next chapter, the wise man says, *"House and wealth are an inheritance from fathers, but a prudent wife is from the Lord"* (19:14). One who finds such a blessing *"obtains favor from the Lord."* God instituted marriage in the beginning (Genesis 2:18-24). Therefore, all blessings that come from the marriage relationship are possible because of

God's perfect plan for man and woman.

> *"A gracious woman attains honor, and ruthless men attain riches"* (11:16).

The *"gracious woman"* is contrasted here with *"ruthless men."* These men have already been discussed under the topic of *obtaining wealth*. The word *"ruthless"* denotes one who is terrifying, powerful, tyrannical, and even oppressive of others. The *"gracious woman"* is the opposite of this, in that she displays kindness toward others and does not seek to elevate herself at the expense of others. This is the type of woman who is worthy of honor and is therefore to be sought after by one who is wisely seeking a wife.

> *"As a ring of gold in a swine's snout so is a beautiful woman who lacks discretion"* (11:22).

Those in the world (and many among God's people, sadly) often place a great deal of emphasis upon physical appearance. Though a woman's appearance may be the first thing one would notice about her, it should not be the basis of judging the quality of her character. At the end of the book of Proverbs when the excellent wife is described, nothing is said about her appearance aside from mentioning a few materials that would be used to make clothing. But there is this warning: *"Charm is deceitful and beauty is vain"* (31:30). Beauty is fleeting and should not be our basis for passing judgment upon anyone. A woman may be beautiful on the outside; but if she *"lacks discretion,"* meaning she exercises poor judgment in failing to carry out her obligations before God, then her beauty is like *"a ring of gold in a swine's snout."* The ring of gold may be beautiful in itself, but it cannot make an ugly pig beautiful. In the same way, a woman's outward appearance may be beautiful; but her physical appearance cannot make her wicked and worldly character attractive to one who values spiritual things and divine wisdom.

> *"The wise woman builds her house, but the foolish tears it down with her own hands"* (14:1).

This verse describes the difference between *encouragement* and *discouragement*. The wise woman – one who would make a good wife – is encouraging to others and seeks to build them up. The foolish woman – one who would make a poor wife – tears down others and is a discouragement to them.

> *"It is better to live in a corner of a roof than in a house shared with a contentious woman"* (21:9).

> *"A constant dripping on a day of steady rain and a contentious woman are alike; he who would restrain her restrains the wind, and grasps oil with his right hand"* (27:15-16).

Peter spoke of the *"holy women"* who lived long ago who were *"submissive to their own husbands; just as Sarah obeyed Abraham, calling him lord"* (1 Peter 3:5-6). God has placed the responsibility of submission upon women from the beginning when he created Eve to be *"a helper suitable for"* Adam (Genesis 2:18). The *"contentious woman"* is the opposite of the submissive wife. She is like the *"constant dripping on a day of steady rain"* by being a source of regular aggravation for him. Through the nagging, bickering, ridicule, antagonism, and strife she forces her husband to endure, she makes it so that he might think that he would be better off living *"in a corner of a roof"* (21:9; 25:24) or *"in a desert land"* (21:19), rather than with her. A contentious woman makes it so that it is impossible to have harmony in the home because she arrogantly wants her way rather than submitting to her husband as his *"help meet"* (Genesis 2:18, KJV).

> *"Drink water from your own cistern and fresh water from your own well. Should your springs be dispersed abroad, streams of water in the streets? Let them be yours alone and not for strangers with you. Let your fountain be blessed, and rejoice in the wife of your youth. As a loving hind and a gracious doe, let her breasts satisfy you at all times; be exhilarated always with her love. For why should you, my son, be exhilarated with an adulteress and embrace the bosom of a foreigner?"* (5:15-20).

God designed marriage as the relationship in which a man and a woman can fulfill their sexual desires (Genesis 2:24; Hebrews 13:4). Solomon's advice to his son in these verses is that he should be *content* with his wife in regard to their sexual relationship (5:15). He was not to seek out the adulteress (5:20); we have already noticed warnings about her in other passages (5:1-14; 6:24-35; 7:1-27; 9:13-18). He warns his son not to let his *"springs be dispersed abroad"* (5:16), dividing his attention, support, care, and affections between his wife (to whom they should exclusively be directed) and others. He says, *"Let your fountain be blessed"* (5:18). A *fountain* refers to a *source*. In this context, it is the source of his life, which is his heart (cf. 4:23). His heart and his life will be blessed as he rejoices *"in the wife of* [his] *youth"* (5:18). He is to enjoy their sexual relationship and *"be exhilarated always with her love"* (5:19). Pursuing sexual desires outside of marriage only leads to trouble. Fulfilling sexual desires within marriage, as God intended, is a great blessing.

The Character of the Excellent Wife

Many read the passage in Proverbs 31 of the *"excellent wife"* or the *"virtuous woman"* (KJV) and assume that the wise man is describing the ideal woman who does not exist in reality. However, even though culture and technology have changed since the time of the book of Proverbs, the *"excellent wife"* today is going to have the same focus as the one described in the following passage – fearing God, supporting her husband, serving her family, and helping others. There can be no change in culture or technology that would rightly call for a shift in focus from these four fundamental areas. Rather than think of the *"excellent wife"* of Proverbs 31 as an ideal that only exists in abstract terms, women today must look at her and see how they might imitate her in their lives.

> *"An excellent wife, who can find? For her worth is far above jewels. The heart of her husband trusts in her, and he will have no lack of gain. She does him good and not evil all the days of her life.*
>
> *"She looks for wool and flax and works with her hands in delight. She is like the merchant ships; she brings her food from afar. She rises while it is still night and gives food to her household and portions to her maidens. She considers a field and buys it; from her earnings she plants a vineyard. She girds herself with strength and makes her arms strong. She senses that her gain is good; her lamp does not go out at night. She stretches out her hand to the*

distaff, and her hand grasps the spindle. She extends her hand to the poor, and she stretches out her hands to the needy. She is not afraid of the snow for her household, for all her household are clothed with scarlet. She makes coverings for herself; her clothing is fine linen and purple. Her husband is known in the gates, when he sits among the elders of the land. She makes linen garments and sells them, and supplies belts to the tradesmen. Strength and dignity are her clothing, and she smiles at the future. She opens her mouth in wisdom, and the teaching of kindness is on her tongue. She looks well to the ways of her household, and does not eat the bread of idleness.

"Her children rise up and bless her; her husband also, and he praises her, saying: 'Many daughters have done nobly, but you excel them all.' Charm is deceitful and beauty is vain, but a woman who fears the Lord, she shall be praised. Give her the product of her hands, and let her works praise her in the gates" (31:10-31).

"An excellent wife, who can find? For her worth is far above jewels" (31:10). In asking the question – *"Who can find?"* – the wise man is not saying that *"an excellent wife"* cannot be found. Rather, he is emphasizing the fact that such a wife is *rare* and is therefore *"worth...far above jewels."* Therefore, because she is so valuable, she ought to be treated as such.

"The heart of her husband trusts in her, and he will have no lack of gain. She does him good and not evil all the days of her life" (31:11-12). As a suitable *"help meet"* (Genesis 2:18,

KJV), the *excellent wife* seeks to support her husband, rather than selfishly pursue her own ambitions and desires. Because of her consistency in this, her husband is able to *trust in her*; and he will prosper. One of her primary focuses is that she *"does him good and not evil all the days of her life."*

"She looks for wool and flax and works with her hands in delight" (31:13). Clarke points out that the wool and flax this woman seeks for her work is not ready woven cloth but the raw material that has likely come from her own flocks and fields. This suggests that the *excellent wife* is willing to work harder, rather than take short cuts, when it is prudent to do so. She is not only able but *willing* to work with her hands. She does so not grudgingly but with joy.

"She is like merchant ships; she brings her food from afar" (31:14). The merchant ships would be engaged in buying, selling, and trading. The *excellent wife* is like them in that she is able to obtain food for her household through the goods she produces that she is able to bring to the market (cf. 31:24). She is also willing to bring *"food from afar,"* signifying the fact that her thoughts revolve around what is best for her family, not what is most convenient for her.

"She rises also while it is still night and gives food to her household and portions to her maidens" (31:15). The fact that the *excellent wife* has maidens (servants) who work for her should not lead us to discount all the work that she does as being non-applicable to women today. In fact, we see that the *excellent wife* makes the most of her time in that she *"rises...while it is still night"* and sees to it that these maidens have the provisions (*food*) and assignments (*portions*) they will need for the day ahead.

"She considers a field and buys it; from her earnings she plants a vineyard" **(31:16).** Earlier the wise man says that this woman's husband *"trusts in her, and he will have no lack of gain"* (31:11). The *excellent wife* is willing to spend money. Yet she does not spend money selfishly on her own desires. Instead, she carefully considers a field and buys it as an investment to contribute to the family. *"She plants a vineyard"* from the money she earns through the sale of those products she makes with her own hands (31:24).

"She girds herself with strength and makes her arms strong" **(31:17).** E. M. Zerr's comments on this verse are helpful: "This woman puts a belt around her waist, not for show or ornament, but to assist her in her work for the family." She *"makes her arms strong"* so that she will be ready and able to carry out the various tasks that are necessary in taking care of her household.

"She senses that her gain is good; her lamp does not go out at night" **(31:18).** The *excellent wife* sees profit in the work that she does. With this positive outlook, she carries out her responsibilities, even though it often means working long hours – into the night – to care for her house.

"She stretches out her hands to the distaff, and her hands grasp the spindle" **(31:19).** This is connected with the verse earlier that describes the *excellent wife* as looking *"for wool and flax and* [working] *with her hands in delight"* (31:13).

"She extends her hand to the poor, and she stretches out her hands to be needy" **(31:20).** This woman is not only concerned with her family. She is also eager to help those who are less fortunate. Because of the work that she does, she is in a

position to provide aid for them.

"She is not afraid of the snow for her household, for all her household are clothed with scarlet. She makes coverings for herself; her clothing is fine linen and purple" **(31:21-22).** The *excellent wife* makes preparations so that her household is well-equipped to handle even challenging circumstances. *"She is not afraid of the snow"* because she prepares for it. The wise man specifically mentions her making clothing for herself. She also supplies clothing for her household, either by making it herself or by obtaining it through the fruit of her labor.

"Her husband is known in the gates, when he sits among the elders of the land" **(31:23).** Being *"known in the gates"* and sitting *"among the elders of the land"* is an indication that her husband is in a place of honor and respect. This is made possible, in part, by having a good *"help meet"* (Genesis 2:18, KJV) who very capably fulfills her responsibilities within the home so that he can focus on his responsibilities outside of the home.

"She makes linen garments and sells them, and supplies belts to the tradesmen" **(31:24).** This woman is more than willing to contribute to her household's income. She does so, not by leaving the home to find work elsewhere, but by doing work that is an extension of the work she is already doing within her role in the home (cf. 31:13, 19, 21-22).

"Strength and dignity are her clothing, and she smiles at the future" **(31:25).** The clothing mentioned here is figurative and describes her character. Because of her character, industriousness, and wise stewardship, she is able to look optimistically toward the future. As the wise man later

mentions the fact that she *"fears the Lord"* (31:30), we can also conclude that this optimism she has is rooted in her faith in God.

"She opens her mouth in wisdom, and the teaching of kindness is on her tongue" (31:26). The *excellent wife* is not only busy working with her hands and taking care of the needs of her household, she is also active in teaching others. The wisdom she teaches is not worldly wisdom, but the wisdom that comes from above. She also teaches kindness, which ought to be expected, given how she treats others.

"She looks well to the ways of her household, and does not eat the bread of idleness" (31:27). Most of this passage about the *excellent wife* describes how the she focuses on her household. This is one of her primary concerns. There are many responsibilities that come with this; so as she *"looks well to the ways of her household,"* she is diligent in her labor. The stereotype of the lazy housewife is nothing like the woman of this passage.

"Her children rise up and bless her; her husband also, and he praises her, saying: 'Many daughters have done nobly, but you excel them all'" (31:28-29). As her focus is largely directed toward her household, particularly her husband and children, these are the ones who rise up to bless and praise her. Her husband recognizes that when compared with other women, she *excels them all*. She is a rare treasure (31:10); and he recognizes this, as every husband of an *excellent wife* should as well.

"Charm is deceitful and beauty is vain, but a woman who fears the Lord, she shall be praised" (31:30). The world values charm and beauty. Yet for one to appreciate this *excellent wife*, he must understand what is truly important. Charm only deceives one into believing that someone is better than her character would indicate. Physical beauty means little. But this woman is worthy of praise because she *"fears the Lord."* Though her service to God is barely mentioned in this passage, all the work that she does in supporting her husband, serving her family, and helping others indicates that she has a strong desire to serve the Lord and fulfill the responsibilities He has given her in the role of a wife and mother.

"Give her the product of her hands, and let her works praise her in the gates" (31:31). The *excellent wife* is worthy of honor, respect, and gratitude for all the work that she does. This praise is not private, and certainly not unspoken. Instead, the praise she is due ought to be public (*"in the gates"*) so that all can recognize her devotion and follow her godly example.

The Application of Wisdom

Family

The first and primary human relationship was that of the man and woman in marriage (Genesis 2:18-24). From this relationship came the first children (Genesis 4:1-2); and all mankind descended from there (Acts 17:26). The book of Proverbs contains several instructions about family relationships, emphasizing the importance of harmony in the home, as well as responsibilities of parents, children, and grandparents.

Harmony in the Home

> *"Better is a dish of vegetables where love is than a fattened ox served with hatred"* (15:17).

> *"Better is a dry morsel and quietness with it than a house full of feasting with strife"* (17:1).

A poor family is able to sustain itself on little more than a *"dish of vegetables"* and a *"dry morsel."* While such a condition may not be desirable in itself, Solomon makes the point that if there is *love* and *quietness* (the absence of strife) within a home, poverty can be endured. More than that, the prosperity that allows one to enjoy *feasting* is not worth pursuing if it leads to *hatred* and *strife* within the home. Too many people sacrifice family in order to pursue success in the things of this life. But no amount of this world's wealth can replace the blessing of harmony in the home.

> *"A wise son makes a father glad, but a foolish son is a grief to his mother"* (10:1).

> *"A foolish son is a grief to his father and bitterness to her who bore him"* (17:25).

A foolish son, by rejecting the ways of wisdom and being concerned only with fulfilling his desires, will cause trouble in the home. He causes grief to both father (17:25) and mother (10:1). By his selfish and rebellious actions, he demonstrates that he *"despises his mother"* (15:20). Rather than helping to preserve harmony in the family, the foolish son instead brings about *"destruction"* (19:13).

> *"He who sires a fool does so to his sorrow, and the father of a fool has no joy"* (17:21).

The joy that accompanies the birth of a child does not always last. As the child grows, if he does not follow the path of wisdom, heeding the instruction of his parents, the *"foolishness"* that is *"bound up in* [his] *heart"* (22:15) will take root and will define his life. One is not a fool from conception or birth but becomes one as he chooses the paths of wickedness. The father of such a one loses the joy he once experienced on account of his child, and it is replaced with sorrow.

> *"My son, if your heart is wise, my own heart also will be glad; and my inmost being will rejoice when your lips speak what is right"* (23:15-16).

> *"The father of the righteous will greatly rejoice, and he who sires a wise son will be glad in him. Let your father and your mother be glad, and let her rejoice who gave birth to you"* (23:24-25).

In contrast with the verse noted previously about the fool causing sorrow (17:21), a son brings joy to his parents when he is *wise* (23:15), when he *speaks what is right* (23:16), and when he practices *righteousness* (23:24). The apostle John, though he spoke of children in the figurative sense, expressed the same joy that Solomon speaks about: *"I have no greater joy than this, to hear of my children walking in truth"* (3 John 4).

> *"Be wise, my son, and make my heart glad, that I may reply to him who reproaches me"* (27:11).

Solomon notes again that a wise son brings joy to his father (cf. 23:15-16, 24-25). In addition to this, he says that when his son walks in wisdom, he is able to *"reply to him who reproaches me."* Whether it is fair or not, the actions of a child affect the reputation of his parent. A son who acts wisely helps to preserve his father's reputation before his fellow man.

To the Parents

> *"A righteous man who walks in his integrity—how blessed are his sons after him"* (20:7).

When one follows God as he ought to, not only will he be blessed (cf. 11:3-8), but his children will be blessed as well. First of all, as God *delights* in those who follow Him, a secondary benefit is that *"the descendants of the righteous will be delivered"* (11:20-21). Second, the children of the righteous man are blessed in that they have his good example to follow. Third, the children of the righteous man are blessed because they are taught by him *"in the way [they] should go"* (22:6).

> *"Train up a child in the way he should go, even when he is old he will not depart from it"* (22:6).

This statement is one that is *generally* true. Certainly, because man has free will, it is possible for parents to teach their children as they ought to and then, when their children have grown, they forsake the paths of righteousness. But generally speaking, when parents lead their children in the way of truth, they will continue in it in their adult life. So the influence of the parents is not limited to the home prior to the children reaching adulthood. Therefore, parents must seriously consider their responsibility in teaching their children.

> *"Foolishness is bound up in the heart of a child; the rod of discipline will remove it far from him"* (22:15).

Foolishness is used two different ways in the book of Proverbs. It can refer to the state of merely *lacking* knowledge. It can also refer to the state of *willful rejection* of knowledge. The former is the type of foolishness in the heart of a child. A child simply *lacks* knowledge and needs to be trained. Part of this training involves discipline. This is not referring to verbal reprimands – though there are times when verbal instruction is necessary – but *corporal punishment*. Solomon makes this clear because he does not just mention *discipline* but the *"rod of discipline."*

> "He who withholds his rod hates his son, but he who loves him disciplines him diligently" (13:24).

Those who refuse to use *corporal punishment* in the discipline of children believe they are acting in love. Yet Solomon says that the one who *"withholds his rod"* – by failing to administer this type of discipline – *"hates his son."* Therefore, the one who loves his son will discipline him *diligently*. The word translated *diligently* means to seek *early* or *earnestly*. The point is that while parents must discipline their children in earnest, they must also do so in a timely manner. This means that from an early age, parents ought to discipline their children appropriately so that the children learn early in life that there are consequences for failing to obey.

> "Discipline your son while there is hope, and do not desire his death" (19:18).

Solomon says that discipline must be administered *"while there is hope."* The implication is that the time may come when there is no hope. The age in which a child's heart becomes hardened and unreceptive to the instruction of his parents will vary. Parents should then discipline their children *diligently* – earnestly and early [see comments on 13:24] – so that this point is never reached. The New American Standard version says: *"Do not desire his death."* This suggests that discipline must always be done in love as an effort to train a child, not as a reaction in anger. The King James Version is worded a little differently: *"Let not thy soul spare for his crying."* The type of discipline that Solomon refers to here (*corporal punishment*) will often result in the child *crying*. Parents should not allow this to deter them in their efforts to administer proper discipline. Solomon explains this in the following verse.

> *"Do not hold back discipline from the child, although you strike him with the rod, he will not die. You shall strike him with the rod and rescue his soul from Sheol"* (23:13-14).

The discipline that Solomon talks about, though it is designed to inflict pain, will not result in serious injury or death. Therefore, though the child may cry (cf. 19:18), a parent should *"not hold back discipline."* God designed children's bodies to be able to withstand corporal punishment. The wise man explains why parents must not refrain from inflicting temporary pain in the discipline of their child – they might *"rescue his soul from Sheol."* The purpose of discipline is not just so a child will learn to respect and obey his parents. It is also so that the child, as he grows, learns to respect and obey the One whom his parents also respect and obey – God.

> *"The rod of reproof gives wisdom, but a child who gets his own way brings shame to his mother"* (29:15).

A child gains wisdom as his parents discipline him as they should. But the child who is spoiled and only gets what he wants and is never disciplined *"brings shame to his mother."* This child never learns limits, boundaries, or reality. Therefore, as he grows older and continues to act according to his own foolish and childish will – because it has never been driven from him (cf. 22:15) – he becomes a source of shame for those who raised him.

> *"Correct your son, and he will give you comfort; he will also delight your soul"* (29:17).

When parents administer discipline to their child, the child will likely not seem to appreciate it. Yet as he grows older, he will come to appreciate the diligence of his parents in this regard. The Hebrew writer noted: *"All discipline for the moment seems not to be joyful, but sorrowful; yet to those who have been trained by it, afterwards it yields the peaceful fruit of righteousness"* (Hebrews 12:11). A disciplined child may later provide *comfort* or *rest* (KJV) to his parents and *"delight"* their souls. From both a temporal and spiritual perspective, parents will find joy in the righteousness of their child. But discipline and correction are necessary for this to happen.

To the Children

> *"A servant who acts wisely will rule over a son who acts shamefully, and will share in the inheritance among brothers"* (17:2).

This verse could be used to emphasize the hard work and dedication of the servant. However, there is another point to be made about the son that Solomon mentions. The fact that he is a son does not mean that his shameful actions will be overlooked. Being a son does not mean that one should feel entitled to anything that his parents have. Solomon specifically mentions the inheritance in this verse. While it is often true that a child will receive an inheritance from his parents, he should not act as though he has an exclusive right to what does not yet belong to him. Too many young people in our society develop an unhealthy sense of *entitlement*. Yet parents can use their resources as they see fit – even by leaving an inheritance to a wise servant. Rather than having a sense of entitlement, children of all ages should learn *humility*, walk *righteously*, and *honor* their parents.

> "He who robs his father or his mother and says, 'It is not a transgression,' is the companion of a man who destroys" (28:24).

This verse also deals with the entitlement mentality that many children have. They believe that they *deserve* whatever might belong to their parents, even before their parents might decide to freely give anything to them. So these wicked children feel as though they can *rob* their parents without doing anything wrong. The wise man notes how serious this crime is when he says that the one who would do this is *"the companion of a man who destroys."*

> "He who assaults his father and drives his mother away is a shameful and disgraceful son" (19:26).

One who would arrogantly mistreat his parents is worse than a stranger who would treat them the same way. The son, as a reflection upon his parents [see comments on 27:11], brings shame and disgrace to them in addition to whatever physical pain he inflicts.

> "There is a kind of man who curses his father and does not bless his mother" (30:11).

> "The eye that mocks a father and scorns a mother, the ravens of the valley will pick it out, and the young eagles will eat it" (30:17).

The most fundamental command for children is the fifth of the Ten Commandments: *"Honor your father and your mother, that your days may be prolonged in the land which the Lord your God gives you"* (Exodus 20:12). With this command came the promise that God would bless them in the land they were receiving. The verses above explain that those who fail to honor their parents will not only miss out on the blessings that come from obedience to this command but will suffer a disgraceful punishment for their sins.

To the Grandparents

> *"Grandchildren are the crown of old men, and the glory of sons is their fathers"* (17:6).

A crown is a sign that one is deserving of honor and respect. Having grandchildren is also a sign that one is worthy of such honor and respect. In order to have grandchildren, a grandparent must first raise his own children in such a way that they are capable of raising their children (his grandchildren).

> *"A good man leaves an inheritance to his children's children, and the wealth of the sinner is stored up for the righteous"* (13:22).

This verse is not talking about a guaranteed outcome. One may be a good man, but on account of circumstances beyond his control, has nothing to leave as an inheritance to his children, let alone his grandchildren. Instead, this verse is talking about the fact that a good man will have the necessary characteristics that might allow him to leave an inheritance to his grandchildren – hard work, good stewardship, and a concern for future generations. Circumstances in life may not always work out as one would hope, but all men ought to have these qualities.

The Application of Wisdom

Friendship

Beyond the family, the next closest relationship that one has is with his friends. The companions with whom one chooses to associate have a great influence upon his thinking and behavior. Therefore, it is important for one to choose his friends wisely. The book of Proverbs contains instructions that will help us see the reason why good friends are so important and why bad friends are so dangerous.

The Value of Good Friends

> *"A friend loves at all times, and a brother is born for adversity"* (17:17).

Because of the family ties that exist, a brother can often be counted upon in times of adversity. On the other hand, a friend – the companion one has by *choice*, rather than by *birth* – can be counted upon for support and encouragement *"at all times,"* not just during times of hardship. It should be noted that the *friend* of this verse is a *true friend*. Sadly, many "friends" are not. These will be discussed later on.

> *"Faithful are the wounds of a friend, but deceitful are the kisses of an enemy"* (27:6).

Because we are imperfect, we often need correction. The wounds of a friend are *"faithful"* because they are designed to correct and guide one back to the truth. Unlike the friend, one's enemy does not have his best interest at heart. Therefore, the *"kisses"* that the enemy offers – signs of affection, approval, and encouragement – are *"deceitful"* because they give one the impression that he is fine in his current state. Though the *"wounds of a friend"* may be temporarily painful, they are ultimately helpful as they allow one to see his sin and make correction. A true friend is willing to do this, rather than attempting to make one feel comfortable in sin as the enemy does.

> *"Oil and perfume make the heart glad, so a man's counsel is sweet to his friend"* (27:9).

The *"counsel"* being offered is teaching or advice. A friend ought to be willing to offer his counsel at times when it will be helpful. Once this counsel is offered, one must recognize the value of the advice given by his friend and take heed to it.

> *"Iron sharpens iron, so one man sharpens another"* (27:17).

One of the things that good friends do for one another is that they help make each other better. A good friend is not going to encourage one to remain in sin or to be content with mediocrity. Instead, a good friend is going to encourage one to become more like God and continue to follow the path of wisdom.

The Danger of Bad Friends

Compared to the passages that discuss the value of good friends, there are many more that warn about the danger of bad friends. A possible reason for this is that man generally understands that friendship is important but is not always as discerning in choosing his friends as he ought to be. Therefore, a greater emphasis is placed upon the warnings. So let us consider the warnings in the book of Proverbs about bad friendships.

> *"Do not be envious of evil men, nor desire to be with them; for their minds devise violence, and their lips talk of trouble"* (24:1-2).

We are not to envy evil men because their ultimate fate is one of destruction when the time comes for God to *"render to man according to his work"* (24:12). In addition to this warning, Solomon says that we should not *"desire to be with them"* because of their corrupt thoughts, speech, and, by implication, actions. Friends are those close companions we *choose* for ourselves. It is imperative that we be very careful not to choose those who are evil.

> *"Leave the presence of a fool, or you will not discern words of knowledge"* (14:7).

Those with whom we associate will have an influence upon us. The longer we associate with fools, the more likely we will start seeing things from their perspective. As fools *"despise...wisdom"* (23:9), we will, on account of their influence, cease discerning the words of knowledge as well.

> *"Let a man meet a bear robbed of her cubs, rather than a fool in his folly"* (17:12).

Solomon uses an example of an obviously dangerous situation (meeting a bear robbed of her cubs) to warn of the danger that is often not as obvious – that of meeting *"a fool in his folly."* Both should be avoided as they can lead to destruction. Interestingly, the obvious danger of the bear can only inflict *physical* harm. The less obvious danger – at least to those who fail to heed the warnings of the wise man – of the fool can inflict both *physical* harm and, worse, *spiritual* harm.

> *"Do not associate with a man given to anger; or go with a hot-tempered man, or you will learn his ways and find a snare for yourself"* (22:24-25).

This verse makes the same warning as one previously considered (14:7). Those with whom we associate will have an influence upon us. Whereas the previous verse warned about the *fool*, this passage warns about the *"man given to anger."* Though their specific sins may be different, the threat is the same. If we *"associate with a man given to anger,"* we *"will learn his ways,"* which will only lead to trouble for us later.

> *"My son, fear the Lord and the king; do not associate with those who are given to change, for their calamity will rise suddenly, and who knows the ruin that comes from both of them?"* (24:21-22).

In choosing one's companions, it is important to do so in the fear of God. Solomon couples this with the fear one ought to have for the king. Because of this connection, we must understand this ruler to be one who is ruling according to the will of God. This is why he says, *"Do not associate with those who are given to change."* Change can be good, particularly if sin and corruption need to be corrected. If rulers are acting contrary to the will of God, we ought to desire change in this regard. But change for the sake of change – which is what Solomon is referring to here – is not good. It reflects an attitude of rebellion and discontent. Seeking change for these reasons, rather than for principles of righteousness, will lead one not only to resist civil leaders, but God as well. Those who have such a rebellious and discontented heart will face calamity *"suddenly."* Therefore, one who is following the path of wisdom will avoid *"those who are given to change."*

> *"He who keeps the law is a discerning son, but he who is a companion of gluttons humiliates his father"* (28:7).

Solomon contrasts *keeping the law* with *keeping company with gluttons*. The glutton is one who lacks self-control. Self-control is necessary to do what is right and keep the law, whether the laws of men or the law of God. One who keeps company with gluttons, learns their intemperate ways, and acts rebelliously as a result will bring shame upon his father.

> *"He who is a partner with a thief hates his own life;*
> *he hears the oath but tells nothing"* (29:24).

When one partners with a thief, he does so by his own free will; he is not forced to do so. Though he may decide to make such a partnership because he hopes to share in the spoil (cf. 1:13-14), in the end, he will only face destruction (1:19). In order to protect himself and his evil partner, he will *tell nothing*, which is in direct violation to the law of God: *"Now if a person sins after he hears a public adjuration to testify when he is a witness, whether he has seen or otherwise known, if he does not tell it, then he will bear his guilt"* (Leviticus 5:1).

> *"Do not eat the bread of a selfish man, or desire his delicacies; for as he thinks within himself, so he is. He says to you, 'Eat and drink!' But his heart is not with you. You will vomit up the morsel you have eaten, and waste your compliments"* (23:6-8).

Those who are selfish may still show kindness to others. But they will be resentful of it. Though the actions of the *"selfish man"* may mask his intentions, Solomon says, *"For as he thinks within himself, so he is."* Friendship with such a selfish individual is not reciprocal – *"his heart is not with you."* Any kindness you give to him – such as a *compliment* – is *wasted*.

> *"He who goes about as a slanderer reveals secrets, therefore do not associate with a gossip"* (20:19).

One who is a gossip does not necessarily say things that are untrue. Rather, a gossip *"reveals secrets"* that should not be made known publicly. Associating with a gossip only gives that person more that they can reveal about you to others. We sometimes hear, "If someone gossips *to* you, he will gossip *about* you." This is essentially what Solomon's point is in this verse.

> *"Drive out the scoffer, and contention will go out, even strife and dishonor will cease"* (22:10).

Strife is a fire that needs fuel to continue to burn. Solomon says elsewhere: *"For lack of wood the fire goes out, and where there is no whisperer, contention quiets down"* (26:20). In any contentious environment, there is at least one person who is guilty of fanning the flames of discord. If we are friends with the *scoffer*, we can be assured that contention and strife will abound in our lives.

> *"A man of too many friends comes to ruin, but there is a friend who sticks closer than a brother"* (18:24).

The New American Standard and King James translations are very different for the first half of this verse. One says, *"A man of too many friends comes to ruin"* (NASB). The other says, *"A man that hath friends must shew himself friendly"* (KJV). The point suggested in the King James Version is the one most think of when reading this verse – if one expects to have friends, he must show himself to be friendly to others. This is true. But the wording in the New American Standard suggests that this refers to more than just showing good will toward others. Instead, one who has *"too many friends"* must try to please them all – a nearly impossible task. Therefore, Solomon says this man *"comes to ruin."* On the other hand, there is *"a friend"* (as opposed to *"many friends"*) who *"sticks closer than a brother."* This is a true friend. Friends like this are sometimes difficult to find. But rather than trying to please everyone – which will only result in making everyone unhappy in one way or another – the wise man will recognize who his true friends are, though they may be few, and not allow himself to ruined by all the others.

> *"Wealth adds many friends, but a poor man is separated from his friend"* (19:4).

> *"Many will seek the favor of a generous man, and every man is a friend to him who gives gifts. All the brothers of the poor man hate him; how much more do his friends abandon him! He pursues them with words, but they are gone"* (19:6-7).

The friends discussed in these verses are not like the *"friend who sticks closer than a brother"* (18:24). These are not *true* friends but are only interested in taking advantage of others. This is why they flock to those who are wealthy and generous, but they forsake those who are poor. True friends will show a genuine interest in the *person*, regardless of his economic status.

> *"He who blesses his friend with a loud voice early in the morning, it will be reckoned a curse to him"* (27:14).

This verse teaches us of the need to be considerate of others. The fact that a *blessing* is given is irrelevant if it comes at such a time and in a certain way as to cause stress and annoyance to the one being blessed. We should be thoughtful of others and not assume that every supposed kindness that we might show in every circumstance and in every way will be welcome.

The Power of Peer Pressure

Peer pressure is not a phenomenon that affects only those who are still in their youth. All people, young and old, can be influenced by their peers. This influence could be either good or bad.

> *"He who walks with wise men will be wise, but the companion of fools will suffer harm"* (13:20).

Those who choose to keep company with *"wise men"* will learn from them and become wise themselves. On the other hand, those who choose to keep company with *"fools"* will suffer the fate of fools. Therefore, companions must be chosen carefully. In the following two passages, Solomon warns of the dangerous influence and peer pressure that comes from evil companions.

> *"My son, if sinners entice you, do not consent. If they say, 'Come with us, let us lie in wait for blood, let us ambush the innocent without cause; let us swallow them alive like Sheol, even whole, as those who go down to the pit; we will find all kinds of precious wealth, we will fill our houses with spoil; throw in your lot with us, we shall all have one purse,' my son, do not walk in the way with them.*

> *"Keep your feet from their path, for their feet run to evil and they hasten to shed blood. Indeed, it is useless to spread the baited net in the sight of any bird; but they lie in wait for their own lives. So are the ways of everyone who gains by violence; it takes away the life of its possessors"* (1:10-19).

"My son, if sinners entice you, do not consent" (1:10). Though Solomon says *"if,"* he does not mean that sinners might leave some people alone and not try to influence them. Sinners *will* try to draw others into their ungodly activities. When this happens, the wise man states simply and clearly, *"Do not consent."*

"If they say, 'Come with us, let us lie in wait for blood, let us ambush the innocent without cause; let us swallow them alive like Sheol, even whole, as those who go down to the pit'" (1:11-12). Those who find enjoyment in doing harm to others are not the kind of friends we ought to have. While those who would try to *"entice"* us will often not propose such extreme and aggressive actions, a similar attitude of contempt for one's fellow man is common today. We should avoid those who have such an attitude.

"'We will find all kinds of precious wealth, we will fill our houses with spoil; throw in your lot with us, we shall all have one purse'" **(1:13-14).** In their wicked activities, those who would tempt us will offer a share in the spoils of their sin. This carries with it the idea of *fellowship*. Yet if one wishes to share in the *spoil* of sin, he must also share in the *punishment* of sin (1:19).

"My son, do not walk in the way with them. Keep your feet from their path, for their feet run to evil and they hasten to shed blood" **(1:15-16).** The ones about whom Solomon warns his son are not simply misguided youths who end up in the wrong place at the wrong time. Evil does not just happen to find them; they go out looking for it. Therefore, if one walks *"in the way with them,"* he will find himself in the same trouble.

"Indeed, it is useless to spread the baited net in the sight of any bird; but they lie in wait for their own blood; they ambush their own lives. So are the ways of everyone who gains by violence; it takes away the life of its possessors" **(1:17-19).** Though their intention is to take advantage of and harm others, these wicked ones are ultimately destroying themselves. Sin always tempts one to focus on the short-term gain and ignore the long-term consequences. Often, one can see the long-term consequences if he will simply pay attention. Solomon says, *"It is useless to spread the baited net in the sight of any bird."* Why? The bird will see it and not fall for the trap. But often, sinners foolishly see,

but ignore, the damaging effects of their sin. They will suffer for it. If we consent to go with them (1:10), we will suffer as well.

> *"Do not enter the path of the wicked and do not proceed in the way of evil men. Avoid it, do not pass by it; turn away from it and pass on. For they cannot sleep unless they make someone stumble. For they eat the bread of wickedness and drink the wine of violence. But the path of the righteous is like the light of dawn, that shines brighter and brighter until the full day. The way of the wicked is like darkness; they do not know over what they stumble"* (4:14-19).

"Do not enter the path of the wicked and do not proceed in the way of evil men. Avoid it, do not pass by it; turn away from it and pass on" (4:14-15). These two verses contain six admonitions to keep from following the wicked. (1) *"Do not enter the path of the wicked."* (2) *"Do not proceed in the way of evil men."* (3) *"Avoid it."* (4) *"Do not pass by it."* (5) *"Turn away from it."* (6) *"Pass on."* Obviously, Solomon is trying to strongly impress upon his son the seriousness of peer pressure from the wicked.

"For they cannot sleep unless they do evil; and they are robbed of sleep unless they make someone stumble" (4:16). Some are so corrupt that they feel as though they *need* to do evil. Others who commit sin end up losing sleep because of their guilty conscience. The individuals that Solomon is describing here have seared their conscience to the point that they no longer feel guilty for sin. But more than that, they feel as though they are missing something important when they fail to bring harm to others.

"For they eat the bread of wickedness and drink the wine of violence" (4:17). Bread provides sustenance. Wickedness is what *sustains* the ones about whom Solomon is warning. *"Wine is a mocker"* (20:1), deceiving people and causing them to *"forget what is decreed"* (31:5). The violence that these sinners carry out against others deceives them into thinking that they are greater than others and immune to retaliation. Yet they forget that they are accountable to God and that *"vengeance"* belongs to Him (Deuteronomy 32:35).

"But the path of the righteous is like the light of dawn, that shines brighter and brighter until the full day. The way of the wicked is like darkness; they do not know over what they stumble" (4:18-19). When choosing what path to take, it may seem obvious that the wise choice would be the path that allows one to see where he is going. Yet the pressure of one's peers who are following the path of darkness is so strong that many follow in that way. We must choose our path based upon what God has revealed, not what our peers (or anyone else) try to tempt us to do.

The Application of Wisdom

Neighbors

We have already studied what the book of Proverbs teaches about our relationships with family and friends. But there are many people we interact with on a regular basis that are outside of these relationships. So let us consider the words of wisdom about our dealings with *neighbors*.

Do Good to Others

> *"Do not withhold good from those to whom it is due, when it is in your power to do it. Do not say to your neighbor, 'Go, and come back, and tomorrow I will give it,' when you have it with you"* (3:27-28).

There may be circumstances in which we are simply unable to do good to others. Paul told the Corinthians that God judges one's performance of good works toward others *"according to what a person has, not according to what he does not have"* (2 Corinthians 8:12). But while there are legitimate reasons why a person may not be able to help his neighbor, there are other reasons that are merely excuses. One will always be able to find an excuse for refusing to do good. When we have the ability and opportunity to help others, we ought to just do it.

> *"Do not devise harm against your neighbor, while he lives securely beside you"* (3:29).

Solomon is describing a condition in which one's neighbor has come to trust him and feel safe living by him. In this circumstance, one must not take advantage of his neighbor's trust. We should not be looking for opportunities when others let their guard down around us, allowing us to somehow harm or take advantage of them. We should seek to do good at all times, so that we gain our neighbor's trust and never violate that trust.

> *"The righteous is a guide to his neighbor, but the way of the wicked leads them astray"* (12:26).

The King James Version says, *"The righteous is more excellent than his neighbor."* Being *"more excellent"* – acting with righteousness and wisdom – allows one to be a guide to others. He sets a standard by his righteousness, showing his neighbor, both by words and actions, that path that he ought to take.

> *"A man who flatters his neighbor is spreading a net for his steps"* (29:5).

Flattery is different than a compliment. A compliment is praise that one deserves for his actions, character, or whatever other reason he may be receiving the compliment. Flattery is praise that is *undeserved* and is given with an ulterior motive – to receive some undeserved favor from the one being praised. One who accepts flattery will often be susceptible to being taken advantage of by the one who flatters him.

> "Deliver those who are being taken away to death, and those who are staggering to slaughter, Oh hold them back" (24:11).

It is easy to make a spiritual application from this verse that we should try to save our neighbors from sin and help them avoid judgment. This is certainly something we should do, but this verse must not be limited to that application. Doing good to one's neighbor includes helping him in time of trouble – even in the threat of *death* and *slaughter* – to defend, protect, and save him.

> "Do not rejoice when your enemy falls, and do not let your heart be glad when he stumbles; or the Lord will see it and be displeased, and turn His anger away from him" (24:17-18).

We are not to find joy in the suffering of others. Even when one is suffering on account of his own sin, we are not to rejoice over this. The consequences and punishment for sin are what Solomon refers to in this passage, as he says that our rejoicing may cause God's *"anger* [to] *turn away from him."* More than this, our rejoicing will cause God's anger that was directed at our neighbor to be turned against us. This is implied in this passage but stated explicitly elsewhere: *"He who rejoices at calamity will not go unpunished"* (17:5).

> "Do not say, 'Thus I shall do to him as he has done to me; I will render to the man according to his work'" (24:29).

This passage is the opposite of the well-known "Golden Rule" given by Jesus: *"In everything, therefore, treat people the* same way you want them to treat you, for this is the Law and the Prophets" (Matthew 7:12). Man often has a tendency to retaliate for what someone else has done to him. Yet the one who walks in wisdom will reject this carnal inclination and do good to others, regardless of how he is treated by them.

> *"If your enemy is hungry, give him food to eat; and if he is thirsty, give him water to drink; for you will heap burning coals on his head, and the Lord will reward you"* (25:21-22).

Paul quoted this passage in Romans 12:19-20 to encourage Christians to leave vengeance to God. In that passage, the apostle also quoted from the Law of Moses: *"Vengeance is Mine, and retribution, in due time their foot will slip"* (Deuteronomy 32:35). We should seek to do good to others, rather than take vengeance into our own hands. We can trust in God that He will handle any punishment that is necessary for the transgressor.

> *"When it goes well with the righteous, the city rejoices, and when the wicked perish, there is joyful shouting. By the blessing of the upright a city is exalted, but by the mouth of the wicked it is torn down"* (11:10-11).

The righteousness of one will naturally be a benefit to others, just as a wicked man will be a detriment to others. The reason for this is that the righteous man is not focused solely on being righteous before God. Certainly, he is concerned about this. But in addition to this, he will also have his righteousness on display before others – not as a show for the praise of men but for doing good to others.

> *"Do not forsake your own friend or your father's friend, and do not go to your brother's house in the day of your calamity; better is a neighbor who is near than a brother far away"* (27:10).

The wise man counsels one to not go to his brother *"in the day of calamity."* The reason for this is that his brother is *"far away."* When the need for help is urgent, there is no time to wait for aid that might come from a distant relative. It is better to have *"a neighbor who is near"* who would be able to come to the aid of one in distress. This verse implies that one ought to be willing to provide help to his neighbor when such help is necessary.

> *"He who pampers his slave from childhood will in the end find him to be a son"* (29:21).

Though this verse refers to a *slave*, rather than a *neighbor*, there is an important principle contained in it about how we deal with those who are outside of our families. Doing good to others for an extended period of time will result in a close relationship being built between us and them. One should not treat others poorly, simply because they are not family. We must do good to all, including our neighbors around us.

Seek Peace

> *"He who loves transgression loves strife; he who raises his door seeks destruction"* (17:19).

Solomon connects *transgression* and *strife* with one another. Those who are wicked are the ones who love strife. Therefore, those who are righteous ought to be striving to maintain peace with their fellow man.

> *"The soul of the wicked desires evil; his neighbor finds no favor in his eyes"* (21:10).

Because the wicked man loves transgression and strife (17:19), he is looking for trouble. Therefore, *"his neighbor finds no favor in his eyes."* One who is looking for something to criticize will find it, even if the charge is unfair. In contrast, the righteous man desires peace and good will among his neighbors. Therefore, he will work to maintain peace whenever such is possible.

> *"Keeping away from strife is an honor for a man, but any fool will quarrel"* (20:3).

Just as the wicked man *"desires evil"* and is looking for some reason to be critical of his neighbor (21:10), the fool is looking for some reason to argue with his neighbor. Though there are certainly occasions that warrant honorable discussion and debate, the fool seeks to argue for the sake of arguing. The honorable course is to avoid strife whenever possible.

> *"Do not go out hastily to argue your case; otherwise, what will you do in the end, when your neighbor humiliates you? Argue your case with your neighbor, and do not reveal the secret of another, or he who hears it will reproach you, and the evil report about you will not pass away"* (25:8-10).

Too often, men foolishly desire to make their private quarrel with a neighbor known to others. Yet when we have a complaint against someone in a personal or private matter, we ought to go to that person first and try to resolve the issue. Instead, if we immediately turn our private dispute into a public quarrel, we may be humiliated and receive reproach if we are found to be in the wrong. Better to keep private matters private whenever possible, rather than risk our own reputation and threaten any hope of future peace with our neighbor.

> *"A man of violence entices his neighbor and leads him in a way that is not good"* (16:29).

The *"man of violence"* is one who seeks his neighbor's destruction. Through evil motives and wicked scheming, he *"entices his neighbor"* to follow after him. The *"man of violence"* will be punished by the Lord (3:31-33; 21:7). His neighbor who follows him will suffer the same fate.

> *"A brother offended is harder to be won than a strong city, and contentions are like the bars of a citadel"* (18:19).

It is often very difficult to repair a damaged relationship. Solomon uses the analogy of capturing a strong city to illustrate this point. Though this is a difficult task, it is easier than trying to win back one who has been offended. The *"contentions"* that arise between brethren *"are like the bars of a citadel,"* keeping out those who are unwelcome – such as the offending brother. We should take care not to damage our relationships with others. Often these severed ties are difficult to restore. Sometimes the damage is irreparable.

> *"Let your foot rarely be in your neighbor's house, or he will become weary of you and hate you"* (25:17).

In trying to be good neighbors, some will take it upon themselves to visit and spend time with them to show their neighbors that they value their relationship. Often this is done with the best of intentions, but Solomon offers a word of caution in this verse. What is often done with good intentions can be interpreted much differently by one's neighbor. While it is good to be friendly, we also need to respect the privacy of others and not impose when we are unwelcome. If a neighbor invites us into his home, we must be careful not to overstay our welcome, lest the good feelings he has for us become exhausted and he learns to resent us.

> *"Like one who takes a dog by the ears is he who passes by and meddles with strife not belonging to him"* (26:17).

"One who takes a dog by the ears" provokes the animal to anger and causes it to turn against him when it may have otherwise ignored him. This is the same thing that one does when he takes it upon himself to meddle in the business of others. When the meddling (often thought to be "helpful" by the meddler) is unwelcome, it will cause the ones involved in the strife to turn against him.

> *"Like a madman who throws firebrands, arrows and death, so is the man who deceives his neighbor, and says, 'Was I not joking?'"* (26:18-19).

The word *madman* is from a root word which suggests the idea of being *rabid* or *insane*. Solomon describes one who is not in control of his mind; therefore, the arrows he shoots, rather than hitting a target, will go in random directions, causing damage to people or things that were never intended as targets. One who deceives his neighbor, but afterward claims to have been *"joking,"* will cause far more damage than he intended, damage which cannot be undone.

* * *

There will be times in which a neighbor commits wrong against us. The following passages provide instruction for such cases.

> *"Hatred stirs up strife, but love covers all transgressions"* (10:12).

> *"A hot-tempered man stirs up strife, but the slow to anger calms a dispute"* (15:18).

When a neighbor sins against us, it is important that we respond appropriately. The appropriate response is not to retaliate, as this will only cause the situation to escalate. If we respond with a *hot-temper* and *hatred*, we will only make the strife worse. Instead, we ought to respond with love and patience, hoping to find a peaceful resolution. If a neighbor sins against us, escalating the tensions and strife will only drive our neighbor further into sin. By showing love and patience, we may be able to later influence him toward the ways of God.

* * *

There will also be times in which a neighbor does no wrong to us. However, too often we are tempted to treat him poorly anyway. The following passages warn against doing this.

> *"Do not contend with a man without cause, if he has done you no harm"* (3:30).
>
> *"Do not be a witness against your neighbor without cause, and do not deceive with your lips"* (24:28).
>
> *"Do not slander a slave to his master, or he will curse you and you will be found guilty"* (30:10).
>
> *"He who returns evil for good, evil will not depart from his house. The beginning of strife is like letting out water, so abandon the quarrel before it breaks out"* (17:13-14).

We must not contend with (3:30), be a witness against (24:28), or speak evil against (30:10) anyone *without cause*. Yes, there are times when it is necessary to contend with, testify against, and offer a report against someone. But if someone has done nothing wrong, it is foolish of us to oppose him. By returning *"evil for good"* in this way, we only invite trouble for ourselves, as *"evil will not depart from"* our houses (17:13). Solomon goes on and says, *"The beginning of strife is like letting out water"* (17:14). Once the floodgates are opened by our unjust accusations, it is difficult to correct the situation. If others have done no wrong, we must not turn against them.

Help the Poor

> *"He who despises his neighbor sins, but happy is he who is gracious to the poor"* (14:21).

After noting the passages that speak of our responsibility to do good to others and seek for peace with our neighbors, the first phrase of this verse fits with those ideas. In the second part of this verse, Solomon specifically talks about one's dealings with *"the poor."* One who is gracious will be *happy* (blessed by God).

> *"One who is gracious to a poor man lends to the Lord, and He will repay him for his good deed"* (19:17).

> *"He who is generous will be blessed, for he gives some of his food to the poor"* (22:9).

One who provides help to the poor will rarely receive recompense from those whom he helps. But one who gives to the poor ought not do so with the hope of receiving repayment from him. Instead, in helping the poor he *"lends to the Lord."* God, who is the giver of all good things (cf. James 1:17), will *"repay him for his good deed."* As with many of the proverbs, this is not to be interpreted to mean that if we use some of our money to help the poor then God will return even more money back to us. The blessings that God provides are not limited to financial and material things. God is able to bless us even after this life. Paul later told Timothy to instruct the rich to *"do good, to be rich in good works, to be generous and ready to share, storing up for themselves the treasure of a good foundation for the future, so that they may take hold of that which is life indeed"* (1

Timothy 6:18-19). The *"life indeed"* they were to focus on as their reward for doing good to others was eternal life.

> *"He who shuts his ear to the cry of the poor will also cry himself and not be answered"* (21:13).

This is much like Jesus' point about forgiveness: *"For if you forgive others for their transgressions, your heavenly Father will also forgive you. But if you do not forgive others, then your Father will not forgive your transgressions"* (Matthew 6:14-15). The same principle is used by Solomon in this passage. One who is *"gracious to a poor man"* will be blessed by God (19:17; 22:9). But one who refuses to help when he has the ability and opportunity to do so will be abandoned by God.

> *"He who oppresses the poor taunts his Maker, but he who is gracious to the needy honors Him"* (14:31).

> *"He who mocks the poor taunts his Maker; he who rejoices at calamity will not go unpunished"* (17:5).

Both the acts of *oppressing* and *mocking* the poor are like *taunting* God. Helping the poor honors God (14:31). Rejoicing in the plight of the poor will result in divine punishment. A few chapters later, Solomon makes a related point: *"Do not rob the poor because he is poor, or crush the afflicted at the gate; for the Lord will plead their case and take the life of those who rob them"* (22:22-23). God is a fair, righteous, and omniscient judge. One who abuses the poor will not escape punishment.

> *"He who oppresses the poor to make more for himself or who gives to the rich, will only come to poverty"* (22:16).

This verse mentions two reasons why one might oppress the poor. The first reason is to *"make more for himself"* or *"increase his riches"* (KJV). Though the poor may not have much, one can still enrich himself by taking from them. The second reason is to give *"to the rich."* A possible reason for doing this would be to gain favor with those who are rich and powerful and be able to use those connections for one's own advantage. In either case, the wise man says that such a plan will backfire. Though he tries to become rich through the oppression of others, he *"will only come to poverty."*

> *"A poor man who oppresses the lowly is like a driving rain which leaves no food"* (28:3).

We might expect that *"a poor man"* would naturally sympathize with others in a condition similar to his own. Knowing that they are in similar circumstances, we might expect that he would try to help so that they could mutually benefit from one another. But some who are poor foolishly oppress others who are also poor. Those who do this are like *"a driving rain which leaves no food."* Though rain will often help crops and plants to grow, a strong storm can often do more harm than good. No one is helped by such oppression; instead, they are only harmed. If we find ourselves in poverty, the way to handle that condition is not to oppress others who are also poor in hopes that we might somehow lift ourselves up out of poverty. Instead, we should seek to help others, even in our poverty, so that we might lift one another up and improve the conditions of everyone.

The Application of Wisdom

Government

Given the way people talk about government as it relates to the Scriptures, many might assume that there is very little in the way of instruction regarding government in the book of Proverbs. Yet there are quite a few passages that teach us about government, as well as providing instructions both to those in government and those who are subject to governing authorities. We begin with the following verse:

> *"Righteousness exalts a nation, but sin is a disgrace to any people"* (14:34).

Though this passage is not *specifically* referring to civil government, there are certainly principles that will apply. A nation will be exalted before God due to the righteousness of the people. Therefore, those in authority ought to encourage righteousness. This will be done primarily by directing the force and wrath of government's power toward the wicked and away from the righteous. Solomon also says that sin among the people brings shame upon the nation. Therefore, those in authority should not support or encourage wickedness among the people.

About Government: Its Place and Role

> *"By the transgression of a land many are its princes, but by a man of understanding and knowledge, so it*

endures" (28:2).

E.M. Zerr explained the significance of the *many princes* in his comments on this verse: "A prince is a leading person without official authority as a general thing. Such men are brought into prominence by the misdoings of a country. But one man of substantial kind of knowledge will ensure the state of a nation." These *princes* that arise through the transgressions of the people will threaten the long-term health of the nation. They consume the country's resources while doing nothing to fulfill the government's God-given role. Actual *"understanding and knowledge"* are far more important contributions that one might make for the health of a nation than merely holding some official position.

> *"The fury of a king is like messengers of death, but a wise man will appease it. In the light of a king's face is life, and his favor is like a cloud with the spring rain"* (16:14-15).

The king, in his role as the head of civil authority, holds the power of life and death over the people he rules (cf. 19:12). Unfortunately, this verse says nothing about the justice incumbent on the king in punishing or rewarding his subjects. For this reason, several passages in Proverbs emphasize the need for kings to rule with *justice*. Yet the characteristic that exists in all human government is not *justice*, but *power*.

> *"A king who sits on the throne of justice disperses all evil with his eyes"* (20:8).

Being in a position of power, God expects rulers to establish their thrones on *justice*. If a ruler does this, evil will be dispersed because justice demands that wickedness be punished.

> *"A wise king winnows the wicked, and drives the threshing wheel over them"* (20:26).

One of the primary responsibilities that government has is to punish those who do evil. The King James Version says, *"A wise king scattereth the wicked,"* again emphasizing the fact that a ruler acting according to his divinely-given role will be a cause of fear for those who do evil. On the other hand, this also implies that when a government refuses to punish wickedness as it ought, sin will abound.

> *"There are three things which are stately in their march. Even four which are stately when they walk: The lion which is mighty among beasts and does not retreat before any, the strutting rooster, the male goat also, and a king when his army is with him"* (30:29-31).

The kings with their armies are described as being *"stately in their march."* The fact that they command such a force demands respect. The mention of such military might also reminds us of the responsibility of rulers to *"bear the sword"* (Romans 13:4).

> *"When the wicked rise, men hide themselves; but when they perish, the righteous increase"* (28:28).

> *"When the righteous increase, the people rejoice, but when a wicked man rules, people groan"* (29:2).

The wise man implies that the ones who *"hide themselves"* from wicked rulers are not other wicked persons who deserve punishment. Righteous kings punish the wicked (20:8, 26); wicked kings do not. Instead, wicked kings are a cause of fear to those who do what is right. Therefore, the righteous hide themselves. Interestingly, *"the righteous increase,"* not necessarily when wicked rulers are replaced with righteous rulers, but simply when wicked rulers *"perish."* The righteous are capable of prospering with or without civil authorities over them because of their reliance upon the providence of God [see comments on 27:23-27] and submission to His rule. Yet righteous rulers are still able to be a blessing to the people of a nation (29:2; cf. 28:12).

> *"Loyalty and truth preserve the king, and he upholds his throne by righteousness"* (20:28).

A king who desires his throne to be established must rule with mercy (KJV), truth, and righteousness. Many in positions of power are concerned solely with enriching themselves and care little for the people. Yet a righteous king will remember his obligation before God to follow His instructions and do what is right.

> *"It is the glory of God to conceal a matter, but the glory of kings to search out a matter. As the heavens for height and the earth for depth, so the heart of kings is unsearchable"* (25:2-3).

These verses are discussing different levels of authority. God is able to *"conceal a matter"* because He is over all – including the king. The king might *"search out a matter"*; but even in his position, there are certain things of God that are unknowable to him. Furthermore, the fact that he must *"search out a matter"* reminds us of the fact that the king is only human; he does not have perfect knowledge of everything. Therefore, God in His omniscience is and always will be greater than the king. Then Solomon says, *"The heart of kings is unsearchable."* Just as the king might *"search out"* matters known only to the one who is greater than he is (God), we might *"search out"* matters known only to the king who rules over us. We cannot know the hearts of those in power, any more than we can know the mind of God, unless it is revealed to us.

> *"Take away the wicked before the king, and his throne will be established in righteousness"* (25:5).

Kings are only human. They can be influenced by evil around them. Therefore, if the king is surrounded by wicked advisors, he will act wickedly. If these advisors are removed, wickedness can be avoided. When wickedness is avoided and righteousness is practiced in its place, *"his throne will be established."*

> *"For riches are not forever, nor does a crown endure to all generations"* (27:24).

God's reign is eternal. Human rulers hold power for a short period of time by comparison. Therefore, all men – both in and out of positions of power – need to remember the limitations of civil authority and submit to the one with ultimate authority – God.

Instructions to Those in Government

Moving on from statements *about* government, we will now consider instructions in the book of Proverbs directed specifically toward those in power.

> *"By me kings reign, and rulers decree justice. By me princes rule, and nobles, all who judge rightly"* (8:15-16).

The *"me"* of this passage is *Wisdom* (8:12). This wisdom is not a worldly wisdom but wisdom that comes from above. Those in positions of authority must not rely upon their own wisdom but seek after God's wisdom.

> *"The king gives stability to the land by justice, but a man who takes bribes overthrows it"* (29:4).

Stability is desirable for a nation as it includes the conditions of peace (from threats without and within) and a freedom from want. This is good for the people, but is also good for the rulers as the people remain content under their rule. This stability is made possible through fairness and justice. A ruler must not be able to be bought, as this will overthrow the stability in the land.

> *"If a king judges the poor with truth, his throne will be established forever"* (29:14).

Too often, men will show kindness to those who they believe will be able to reciprocate. For those in positions of power, this means that they pay special regard to those who are rich, powerful, and influential; but the poor are often ignored. Rulers must pay attention to the poor and judge them *"with truth"* as this, not the neglect of the poor in favor of the rich, will cause his throne to be established.

> *"Open your mouth for the mute, for the rights of all the unfortunate. Open your mouth, judge righteously, and defend the rights of the afflicted and needy"* (31:8-9).

This passage is related to the one previously noted (29:14). Those who are unable to defend themselves must be protected by the civil authorities against those who would abuse them. But in all of this, the king must rule *justly* (29:4). The rights of the less fortunate must be defended. However, in defending the rights of the lowly against the rich and powerful, a ruler must not go to the other extreme – attack the rights of the rich in the name of the poor. The Law specifically stated: *"Nor shall you be partial to a poor man in his dispute"* (Exodus 23:3). Showing favoritism – for either the rich or the poor – is a perversion of justice. A ruler must *"defend the rights of the afflicted and needy"* without assaulting the rights of others.

> *"A divine decision is in the lips of the king; his mouth should not err in judgment. A just balance and scales belong to the Lord; all the weights of the bag are His concern. It is an abomination for kings to commit wicked acts, for a throne is established on righteousness"* (16:10-12).

The statement, *"A divine decision is in the lips of the king,"* means that a king ought to rule in such a way that is in harmony with God's law. *"A just balance and scales belong to the Lord"* means that everything that is right, just, and fair is in harmony with His instructions. No human standard that is contrary to God's standard ought to be followed or enforced. Furthermore, when Solomon says, *"It is an abomination for kings to commit wicked acts,"* he is saying that those in authority are not above the law – either God's law or man's. Therefore, rulers must act *righteously* in the fear of God.

> *"Righteous lips are the delight of kings, and he who speaks right is loved"* (16:13).

Rulers are to value truth and righteousness. They are not to be like many who delight in and love those who will flatter and deceive them.

> *"Excellent speech is not fitting for a fool, much less are lying lips to a prince"* (17:7).

"Excellent speech" is not characteristic of a fool. Similarly, *"lying lips"* ought not be characteristic of a prince (or anyone within the government). Unfortunately, *lying* is often associated with those in power (for good reason). But the instruction for those in authority is that they should be truthful and honest in their dealings with others – including the ones under their power.

> *"If a ruler pays attention to falsehood, all his ministers become wicked"* (29:12).

Those who serve the king do so at his pleasure. Therefore, the king is going to surround himself with those who already think like him or who will go along with him in his plans. So if a king *"pays attention to falsehood"* – likely the counsel of a few of his advisors (25:5) – and follows after what is evil, then eventually *"all his ministers become wicked."*

> *"In a multitude of people is a king's glory, but in the dearth of people is a prince's ruin"* (14:28).

Though it would be easy for a ruler to become arrogant because of his position, the wise man reminds him that his *glory* or *honour* (KJV) is only possible because of the people he rules. There are two implications to this. First, without the loyalty of the people, those in power cannot rule, which leads to their downfall. This means that for one to effectively rule over the long-term, he must do so with the consent of the governed. Second, without the life of the people, those in power cannot rule. Therefore, being in a position of civil authority demands that one protect the people from those who would do harm to them.

> *"It is not good to fine the righteous, nor to strike the noble for their uprightness"* (17:26).

We have already noticed the responsibility of rulers to punish evildoers (20:8, 26). However, they must take care not to punish the righteous along with the wicked. Peter would later explain the primary responsibility of civil authorities: *"For the punishment of evildoers and the praise of those who do right"* (1 Peter 2:14). A sloppy execution of punishment that affects the righteous is not good. Those who are righteous and upright should not be fined, struck down, or otherwise harmed by those in power.

> *"Those who forsake the law praise the wicked, but those who keep the law strive with them"* (28:4).

It is assumed in this verse that the law under consideration is just and in harmony with divine precepts. Though there may be some ungodly laws that are created to praise and reward the wicked, those laws that are in harmony with the will of God will be opposed to the wicked. Therefore, if a ruler sides with the wicked, he has forsaken every legitimate law that agrees with divine law. A ruler who fears God and understands the importance of governing according to divine precepts will *"strive (contend, KJV) with"* the wicked.

> *"Like a roaring lion and a rushing bear is a wicked ruler over a poor people. A leader who is a great oppressor lacks understanding, but he who hates unjust gain will prolong his days"* (28:15-16).

Wicked, oppressive rulers will only harm their people. In doing so, they will not *"prolong* [their] *days,"* even though this may be their primary goal. They *lack understanding* in that they fail to see the virtue in doing what God expects of them in their position of authority.

Our Responsibility Toward Government

Most men will not find themselves *in* government, but *subject to* governing authorities. Therefore, it is important that we understand what our responsibility and attitude should be toward those in power.

> *"My son, fear the Lord and the king; do not associate with those who are given to change"* (24:21).

In considering the danger of bad friends, we already noticed that trouble comes when one associates with *"those *who are given to change.*" Sometimes change is necessary, such as when one is changing from a state of wickedness to a state of righteousness. But this verse is warning about those with a rebellious attitude who want change for the sake of change. Some civil authorities will roughly follow God's instructions for them. Others will completely reject God's will for them. Naturally, the righteous man will want stability with the good rulers and change with the evil rulers. However, some are not content no matter who is in charge. They want change when the wicked are in power *and* when the righteous are in power. We are not to keep company with those who have such a rebellious attitude.

> *"He who loves purity of heart and whose speech is gracious, the king is his friend"* (22:11).

Of course, this verse assumes that the king is righteous himself so that he values such qualities. But regardless of the character of the king, we must act with honor and integrity. This is the only right way to gain favor with those in authority. Those who are righteous will take note of it and respond with kindness.

> *"The terror of a king is like the growling of a lion; he who provokes him to anger forfeits his own life"* (20:2).

The king has the power to do harm to those he desires to punish. This may be done properly (punishing evildoers – 20:26) or improperly (oppressing the righteous along with the wicked – 17:26). Regardless of the reason for the wrath that comes from those in power, we should do as Paul told the brethren in Thessalonica: *"Make it your ambition to lead a quiet life"* (1 Thessalonians 4:11). We should not be looking for trouble but should strive to conduct our lives in such a way that those in power – whether righteous or wicked – will leave us alone.

> *"When you sit down to dine with a ruler, consider carefully what is before you, and put a knife to your throat if you are a man of great appetite. Do not desire his delicacies, for it is deceptive food"* (23:1-3).

This passage warns us that not everything that is offered to us by those in power is helpful or good for us. Therefore, if the government offers us *anything*, before agreeing to accept it, we need to carefully consider the potential ramifications of our acceptance. There may be times in which it would be better to refuse what is offered to us than to accept what is offered along with whatever strings are attached to it.

> *"Do not claim honor in the presence of the king. And do not stand in the place of great men; for it is better that it be said to you, 'Come up here,' than for you to be placed lower in the presence of the prince, whom your eyes have seen"* (25:6-7).

We are to exercise humility in the presence of those in power so that if they take notice of us, it is to exalt us and not humble us. Jesus discussed this same principle in Luke 14:7-11.

> *"Many seek the ruler's favor, but justice for man comes from the Lord"* (29:26).

This is possibly the most important verse to remember in the book of Proverbs about our attitude toward civil authorities. Many people seek the favor of rulers because they see these leaders as holding the power of life or death over them (cf. 16:14-15). Yet we must remember that *"justice for man comes from the Lord."* Any justice from civil authorities only comes as they comply with the will of God. Any injustice from civil authorities will one day be made right by God as He is over all, even those who rule over us in this life. Rather than looking to civil authority as our deliverer and the standard of righteousness, we need to look to God for these things. We must never forget the surpassing greatness of God and the inferiority and comparative weakness of human rulers.

The Application of Wisdom

God

The final point of application in our study of Proverbs has to do with God and our relationship to Him. The entire book of Proverbs has been a discussion of the wisdom that comes from above. Of course, the source of this wisdom is God Himself. But without understanding God and our place before Him, it would be difficult for us to find sufficient reason to trust that His way is best and live our lives according to it. Therefore, we must understand God to fully understand the importance of the wisdom contained in this book.

About God

> "The Lord possessed me at the beginning of His way, before His works of old" (8:22).

Wisdom is speaking in this verse. The verses that follow mention God as being *eternal* (8:23) and our *Creator* (8:24-31). The wisdom that has been discussed in the book of Proverbs belongs to Him. He did not have to acquire wisdom as we do. He possessed wisdom before the world was even formed.

> "There is no wisdom and no understanding and no counsel against the Lord" (21:30).

Because wisdom belongs to God (8:22), He is the standard. Therefore, we cannot successfully challenge Him. Job made this same point about God: *"If one wished to dispute with Him, he could not answer Him once in a thousand times"* (Job 9:3).

> *"Many plans are in a man's heart, but the counsel of the Lord will stand"* (19:21).

God's truth is unchanging. Though man has *"many plans,"* none of his ideas will ever rival the wisdom of God that comes down from above.

> *"The eyes of the Lord preserve knowledge, but He overthrows the words of the treacherous man"* (22:12).

"The eyes of the Lord" is a phrase which refers to God's omniscience (15:3; cf. 2 Chronicles 16:9; Jeremiah 16:17; Hebrews 4:13). The Lord is aware of all that goes on among men. For those who love, practice, and teach the truth, He sees them and blesses them in their efforts. On the other hand, God is also aware of *"the words of the transgressor"* (KJV) and destroys him for his labors in opposition to the truth.

> *"Every word of God is tested; He is a shield to those who take refuge in Him. Do not add to His words or He will reprove you, and you will be proved a liar"* (30:5-6).

The word of God has stood the test of time, and man cannot improve upon it. Therefore, one who would attempt to improve upon God's word by adding to it will be *"proved a liar."* Not only is the word of God *right*, but it is *complete*, making additions to it unnecessary. Being complete as it is, His word as a *"shield"* is able to provide the perfect defense and protection for *"those who take refuge in Him."*

> *"The hearing ear and the seeing eye, the Lord has made both of them"* (20:12).

As has already been established, God is the Creator (cf. 8:22-31). But some today, in a foolish attempt to harmonize the fact that God is Creator with the godless theory of evolution, have suggested that God created the universe and set processes in motion that would lead to the evolution of life as we know it (theistic evolution). Yet God did not create the matter and conditions whereby man would eventually evolve from lower forms of life, which evolved themselves from still lower forms of life. Instead, the wise man affirms that God made *"the hearing ear and the seeing eye"* of man

> *"The Lord is far from the wicked, but He hears the prayer of the righteous"* (15:29).

This is similar to what Solomon's father David wrote in the Psalms: *"The eyes of the Lord are toward the righteous and His ears are open to their cry. The face of the Lord is against evildoers, to cut off the memory of them from the earth"* (Psalm 34:15-16; cf. 1 Peter 3:12). While Solomon mentions God being *"far from the wicked,"* David went further and said that God is *"against evildoers."* God, in His justice, will not allow the wicked to go unpunished. Though He may leave them on their own for a time, He will eventually punish them. On the other hand, the righteous enjoy a continued state of God's kindness and watchfulness.

Fear God

> *"The fear of the Lord is the beginning of knowledge; fools despise wisdom and instruction"* (1:7).

Fear is inseparably connected with obedience (cf. Ecclesiastes 12:13; Acts 10:35). Yet in order to obey, one must have knowledge about what to obey. The two sides of fear – respect for God and terror of God – motivate one to find out what God desires of him so that he can obey the Lord's will.

> *"My son, fear the Lord and the king; do not associate with those who are given to change"* (24:21).

We have already cited this verse in connection with friendships and government. It is necessary to include it here as well. We are not to have a heart of rebellion but one of submission to God, rooted in a healthy fear of Him.

* * *

> *"The plans of the heart belong to man, but the answer of the tongue is from the Lord. All the ways of a man are clean in his own sight, but the Lord weighs the motives. Commit your works to the Lord and your plans will be established. The Lord has made everything for its own purpose, even the wicked for the day of evil. Everyone who is proud in heart is an abomination to the Lord; assuredly, he will not be unpunished. By lovingkindness and truth iniquity is atoned for, and by the fear of the Lord one keeps away from evil. When a man's ways are pleasing to the Lord, He makes even his enemies to*

be at peace with him" (16:1-7).

"The plans of the heart belong to man, but the answer of the tongue is from the Lord" **(16:1).** The thoughts and motives of man are wholly his. But truth – the proper *"answer of the tongue"* – is from God. We must always look to God as the source of truth, not to our own hearts. The Lord, through the prophet, reminded us of the danger in following one's heart rather than following Him: *"The heart is more deceitful than all else"* (Jeremiah 17:9).

"All the ways of a man are clean in his own sight, but the Lord weighs the motives" **(16:2).** Man is free to choose his actions and the direction of his life. Each one will do what seems right to him. Yet we must remember: God will hold us accountable for all that we do in this life.

"Commit your works to the Lord and your plans will be established" **(16:3).** We must submit to God. If we do, we will enjoy the blessings that come from obedience to Him.

"The Lord has made everything for its own purpose, even the wicked for the day of evil. Everyone who is proud in heart is an abomination to the Lord; assuredly, he will not be unpunished" **(16:4-5).** This is not teaching that God is meticulously micro-managing every mundane moment of our lives so that everything happens for a reason. Instead, it simply means that the future of all things is in the hands of God. Those who are wicked will one day face punishment. One who arrogantly believes he is exempt from this fate *"is an abomination to the Lord."* As long as he refuses to repent, he will have no hope of escaping the punishment for iniquity that has been determined by God.

"By lovingkindness and truth iniquity is atoned for, and by the fear of the Lord one keeps away from evil" (16:6). The way to avoid the punishment that comes for sin is to follow after *"lovingkindness and truth."* In the fear of the Lord, one will recognize that there is a future judgment in which God will *"render to man according to his work"* (24:12). Knowing this, the one who fears God will avoid sin and do what is right so that he might be prepared to face the Lord in judgment. The one who does not fear God – and, therefore, practices all sorts iniquity – will not have his sins atoned for and will progress further and further into sin.

"When a man's ways are pleasing to the Lord, He makes even his enemies to be at peace with him" (16:7). There is a peace that comes from following after the Lord. This does not mean that a godly man's enemies will have a change of heart necessarily. Rather, it means that by following the ways of God, we might either have a positive influence on others so that they desire to live in peace with us or as we walk in wisdom, the wicked man will find little reason to attack us or rally others against us. Therefore, following after divine wisdom helps lead to peace with others.

* * *

> *"He who walks in his uprightness fears the Lord, but he who is devious in his ways despises Him"* (14:2).

The proof of one fearing the Lord is walking uprightly. Without practicing righteousness, one cannot claim that he truly fears God. Jesus expressed the same principle of obedience proving one's devotion to God: *"If you love Me, you will keep My commandments"* (John 14:15). If we do not keep the

Lord's commandments, our claim that we love Him is baseless. In the same way, if we do not practice righteousness, our claim that we fear God is baseless. If we are *"perverse in [our] ways"* (KJV), we are showing our contempt for God and proving that *"there is no fear of God before [our] eyes"* (Psalm 36:1; cf. Romans 3:18).

> *"The fear of the Lord is to hate evil; pride and arrogance and the evil way and the perverted mouth, I hate"* (8:13).

Many people want to claim to be religious and have faith in God, yet they tolerate, accept, and, in some cases, even practice those things which are evil. If we truly fear God, we will *"hate evil"* as He also does (cf. 6:16-19).

> *"In the fear of the Lord there is strong confidence, and his children will have refuge. The fear of the Lord is a fountain of life, that one may avoid the snares of death"* (14:26-27).

The wise man is not saying that one who fears God has a right to become arrogant. This is not about *arrogance*, but *confidence*. If we fear God, we will understand the need to obey Him and then will actually do it. When we know that we are serving the Lord, we can be confident knowing that we are obeying the truth (His word), that we are avoiding the consequences of sin (*"the snares of death"*), and that we have a hope of a reward from Him (*"a fountain of life"*).

> *"The fear of the Lord leads to life, so that one may sleep satisfied, untouched by evil"* (19:23).

In order to *"sleep satisfied,"* one must have a clear conscience and dwell in security. As we fear and obey God, we can have a clear conscience knowing that we are practicing His will. We can also enjoy security through following His word (cf. 16:7).

> *"Better is a little with the fear of the Lord than great treasure and turmoil with it"* (15:16).

Serving God is more important than anything of this life. As we have considered before, although the book of Proverbs focuses a lot on the blessings of wisdom that can be found in this life, fearing God and following His will are about much more than that. It may be that a godly person will possess *"little"* or experience *"turmoil"* in life. But as long as he fears the Lord, he is better off than one who possesses great wealth but has rejected the Lord.

> *"Do not let your heart envy sinners, but live in the fear of the Lord always."* (23:17).

There will be times when it seems as though sinners are better off than we are. During these times, we may be tempted to *envy* them. But we must not do this. As noted in the previous verse, one who fears the Lord is better off than one who does not, regardless of the earthly peace and prosperity enjoyed by the godless person (15:16). The future of the one who fears God is better than the future of the wicked man. Therefore, we must continually live in the fear of God so that we can please Him in all things.

* * *

Understanding who God is and what He has done should be reason enough to fear (respect) Him. We are to have a balanced fear of the Lord (respect and terror). So that we will be motivated to obey, we must remember our accountability before Him as we will stand before Him in judgment.

> *"For the ways of a man are before the eyes of the Lord, and He watches all his paths"* (5:21).

> *"The eyes of the Lord are in every place, watching the evil and the good"* (15:3).

God is omniscient – He sees and knows all (cf. Hebrews 4:13). There is nowhere to go to hide from the Lord as His *"eyes...are in every place."* There is nothing we can do that would be beyond His awareness, as our *"ways...are before* [His] *eyes...and He watches all* [our] *paths."* Rather than try to hide from the Lord, we should strive to be numbered among those who are good, rather than among those who are evil.

> *"Sheol and Abaddon lie open before the Lord, how much more the hearts of men!"* (15:11).

> *"The spirit of man is the lamp of the Lord, searching all the innermost parts of his being"* (20:27).

Before telling us, *"All things are open and laid bare to the eyes of Him with whom we have to do,"* the Hebrew writer said, *"The word of God is...able to judge the thoughts and intentions of the heart"* (Hebrews 4:12-13). God knows our thoughts and what is in our hearts. It is certainly true that no one among our fellow men can know our thoughts and intentions. Paul wrote, *"For who among men knows the thoughts of a man except the spirit of the* man which is in him?" (1 Corinthians 2:11). But God is different from man. He *"forms the spirit of man within him"* (Zechariah 12:1). Therefore, though we may be able to hide *"the thoughts and intentions of the heart"* from others, it is impossible to hide them from God.

> *"The rich and the poor have a common bond, the Lord is the maker of them all"* (22:2).

Though men may not treat the rich and poor as equals, they are equal before God. God is their Maker. Both have a common origin, and they have been made *"in the image of God"* (Genesis 1:27; cf. Acts 17:26). They also both have a common future. When they die, *"the dust will return to the earth as it was, and the spirit will return to God who gave it"* (Ecclesiastes 12:7). No matter what our temporary circumstances are in this life, we will one day meet our Maker and will have to give an account for what we have done in our lives (cf. Hebrews 9:27; 2 Corinthians 5:10).

> *"The refining pot is for silver and the furnace for gold, but the Lord tests hearts"* (17:3).

The purpose of the refining pot and the furnace was to remove from the silver and gold any impurities that might have been present. God tests our hearts in the same way through the standard found in His revealed word. The goal for us – just as it is with silver and gold – is *purity*. As He tests our hearts, He is determining whether we are worthy of a reward or not.

> *"Every man's way is right in his own eyes, but the Lord weighs the hearts"* (21:2).

Everyone does what he believes to be right. Of course, what one believes to be right is not necessarily going to be right (cf. 14:12; 16:25; Jeremiah 10:23). If everyone were a standard to himself, then all would be justified. But we answer to a higher power – God. He *"weighs the hearts"* (cf. 17:3) to determine whether or not we can stand justified before Him.

> *"If you say, 'See, we did not know this,' does He not consider it who weighs the hearts? And does He not know it who keeps your soul? And will He not render to man according to his work?"* (24:12).

God is concerned with what we *do*. When we stand before Him in judgment, we will be either rewarded or punished based upon our *work* (cf. 2 Corinthians 5:10). There will be no exemptions or excuses in that day. If we fear and obey Him, we will be rewarded. But if we, through our disobedience, demonstrate a lack of fear, we will be punished.

Trust God

> *"Trust in the Lord with all your heart and do not lean on your own understanding. In all your ways acknowledge Him, and He will make your paths straight. Do not be wise in your own eyes; fear the Lord and turn away from evil. It will be healing to your body and refreshment to your bones"* (3:5-8).

Solomon's primary point in this passage is that we must put our trust in God, rather than thinking we can find the path of wisdom apart from Him. But it is important that we put our trust in Him *completely* – with *all* our hearts (3:5) and in *all* our ways (3:6). If we do this, *"He will make* [our] *paths straight."*

This does not mean that whatever we do will be right. We can still choose to do what is wrong. Instead, Solomon's point is that God will direct our steps to whatever degree we acknowledge Him and trust in His ways. We must trust in God in fear (3:7) – knowing that God has the power to destroy us but will not do so as long as we obey Him and *"turn away from evil."* Doing this will lead to our being blessed by God.

> *"The lot is cast into the lap, but its every decision is from the Lord"* (16:33).

This verse does not mean that everything that happens or is decided has been foreordained by God. Solomon also wrote, *"Time and chance overtake them all"* (Ecclesiastes 9:11). The casting of lots was a practice done under the Old Law for matters which required a divine decision (cf. Leviticus 16:7-10). The apostles cast lots to determine who would replace Judas in their number (Acts 1:23-26). It did not produce a random outcome, but a divinely-decreed outcome (it would *"show which one…You have chosen"* – Acts 1:24). It eliminated the influence of man in the decision, thus requiring man to put his trust in God for the decision. Though we should not expect God to reveal His will to us through the casting of lots today, we should trust Him enough to look to what He has revealed – His word – to guide us in our lives.

> *"The name of the Lord is a strong tower; the righteous runs into it and is safe"* (18:10).

There is safety and protection to be found in the Lord. However, this safety is only enjoyed by those who *run to Him* so that they might be protected. We cannot stubbornly refuse to follow God and expect Him to be with us.

> *"The fear of man brings a snare, but he who trusts in the Lord will be exalted"* (29:25).

Trusting in the Lord is contrasted with fearing man. The implication is that when we place our complete trust in the Lord, we then have no reason to fear man. To fear man means one does not have the faith in God that he ought to have. Therefore, when trouble comes, he does not take refuge in the strong tower of the Lord (18:10). Trouble is going to come, regardless of our faith in God. The only way to be *"exalted"* is to keep our trust in Him.

> *"Do not say, 'I will repay evil'; wait for the Lord, and He will save you"* (20:22).

When trouble comes against us from our fellow man, we are to leave vengeance to God (cf. Deuteronomy 32:35; Romans 12:19). Though we may have to *wait* for Him, in the end the salvation that He offers is far greater than whatever vengeance we might be able to obtain for ourselves.

Pleasing God

> *"To do righteousness and justice is desired by the Lord more than sacrifice"* (21:3).

The type of sacrifice mentioned in this verse is the sacrifice that would be offered for sin. God has always given His people an avenue whereby they could obtain forgiveness for their sins. Yet this avenue of forgiveness – whether the sacrifices under the Old Law or the prayers we offer to God today (1 John 1:9; Acts 8:22) – is not to be abused. Though an avenue of forgiveness exists, the first priority of God's people ought to be to avoid sin in the first place (cf. 1 John 2:1). This is why Solomon says that practicing *"righteousness and justice"* is preferable to one needing to seek forgiveness. It is as Samuel told Saul: *"Has the Lord as much delight in burnt offerings and sacrifices as in obeying the voice of the Lord? Behold, to obey is better than sacrifice, and to heed than the fat of rams"* (1 Samuel 15:22).

> *"He who turns away his ear from listening to the law, even his prayer is an abomination"* (28:9).

If one does not obey the Lord, thereby demonstrating a lack of respect for Him, he has no right to expect the Lord to heed him when he prays. Furthermore, the wise man says that the prayer of one who refuses to obey God *"is an abomination."* It is not just that God *ignores* the prayers of the disobedient. These prayers are *offensive* to Him. David also spoke of God's active opposition to the wicked as opposed to some divine indifference: *"The eyes of the Lord are toward the righteous and His ears are open to their cry. The face of the Lord is against evildoers, to cut off the memory of them from the earth"* (Psalm 34:15-16; cf. 1 Peter 3:12).

> *"The sacrifice of the wicked is an abomination to the Lord, but the prayer of the upright is His delight. The way of the wicked is an abomination to the Lord, but He loves one who pursues righteousness"* (15:8-9).

Just as the prayer of the disobedient is offensive to God [see comments on 28:9], *"the sacrifice of the wicked"* is offensive as well [see comments on 21:3]. On the other hand, God *delights* in *"the prayer of the upright."* He wants man to come to Him in prayer, but man must make a sincere effort to please

Him. *"He loves one who pursues righteousness."* The fact that this is a pursuit does not mean that righteousness is unattainable, but rather that righteousness is something which must be continually sought. It requires *action* on man's part; as the apostle John wrote, *"The one who practices righteousness is righteous, just as He is righteous"* (1 John 3:4). But *"the way of the wicked"* – his sinful actions and the ungodly direction of his life – is offensive to the Lord.

> *"Evil plans are an abomination to the Lord, but pleasant words are pure"* (15:26).

In the verses above, Solomon has shown God's contempt for the prayers, sacrifices, and actions of the wicked (28:9; 15:8-9). This verse goes further in saying that *"evil plans are an abomination to the Lord."* God is aware of more than what is visible (our ways, 15:9) and what is directed specifically toward Him (prayers, 28:9; sacrifices, 15:8). Being omniscient, He is aware of our thoughts. If our thoughts are wicked, they are *"an abomination"* to Him. The second phrase of this verse is different in the King James Version. While the New American Standard translation seems to be simply describing a characteristic of *"pleasant words"* (that they are pure), the King James Version makes a clearer contrast with the plans/thoughts of the wicked in the first part of the verse: *"But the words of the pure are pleasant words"* (KJV). God delights in those who are pure and upright. These characteristics will be seen even in one's speech.

> *"The perverse in heart are an abomination to the Lord, but the blameless in their walk are His delight"* (11:20).

This verse contains the same thought as some of the verses previously considered. Those who are corrupt in their heart are offensive to God. Those who obey Him and follow the path of wisdom are pleasing to Him.

> *"He who justifies the wicked and he who condemns the righteous, both of them alike are an abomination to the Lord"* (17:15).

Offending God is not just about what we might do that would be directed specifically toward Him (i.e. prayers and sacrifices – 21:3; 28:9; 15:8). Justifying the wicked and condemning the righteous are also offensive to Him. Doing these things shows a contempt for the law of God (by justifying the wicked) and a contempt for the people of God (by condemning the righteous). We cannot please God if we do not respect His law enough to recognize and acknowledge sin. We also cannot please God if we do not love His people.

Conclusion

Throughout this study, we have seen how God expects His people to grow in wisdom – not wisdom that is of the world, but wisdom that comes from above. As we have gone through this study, we have divided the material in the book of Proverbs into four sections:

1. **The *appeal* of wisdom** – God has not hidden His wisdom so that we cannot find it. He offers it to us. Solomon describes wisdom as *inviting* us to take hold of it. This invitation is open to all, not just to an elite few.
2. **The *appreciation* of wisdom** – When God calls us to take hold of His wisdom, He does not do so without giving us the reasons *why* it is good for us to pursue wisdom. There are blessings that come from following wisdom and negative consequences that come from rejecting wisdom.
3. **The *acquisition* of wisdom** – Once we recognize the *appeal* of wisdom and understand the reasons why we should *appreciate* wisdom, we then need to know how to *acquire* wisdom. With diligence and a proper attitude on our part, we can gain the wisdom that God offers.
4. **The *application* of wisdom** – Wisdom is not just about what we *know*, but what we *do*. Therefore, the bulk of the book of Proverbs (and roughly two-thirds of the material in this study)

focuses on how we are to *apply* wisdom. This will cover every area of our lives – home, work, society, and religion.

Our pursuit and application of wisdom is something that must be done throughout our lives. Our present and future happiness depends upon our remembering this fact.

> *"My son, eat honey for it is good, yes, the honey from the comb is sweet to your taste; know that wisdom is thus for your soul; if you find it, then there will be a future, and your hope will not be cut off"* (24:13-14).

Our *souls* – our entire being, including our existence beyond this life – is benefited by wisdom. By following wisdom, we can look forward in *hope* to a future reward from God. But in order for this hope to be realized, we must not turn back from following wisdom.

> *"Hear, O sons, the instruction of a father, and give attention that you may gain understanding, for I give you sound teaching; do not abandon my instruction"* (4:1-2).

> *"Acquire wisdom! Acquire understanding! Do not forget nor turn away from the words of my mouth"* (4:5).

> *"My son, give attention to my words; incline your ear to my sayings. Do not let them depart from your sight; keep them in the midst of your heart"* (4:20-21).

> *"Let your eyes look directly ahead and let your gaze be fixed straight in front of you. Watch the path of your feet and all your ways will be established. Do not turn to the right nor to the left; turn your foot from evil"* (4:25-27).

Never forget the *appeal* of wisdom, in which God invites you to take hold of the wisdom that has been His since the beginning.

Never forget the need to *appreciate* wisdom, remembering the blessings that come from following wisdom and the pitfalls that come from rejecting it.

Never forget the need to *acquire* wisdom, in humility seeking diligently to obtain it.

Never forget the need to *apply* wisdom, following the will of God in every area and at every age of your life.

I pray that this study has been helpful to you, encouraging you toward more faithful service to God.

Works Referenced

Clarke, A. (2011). *Adam Clarke's Commentary* (Vol. 3) [Kindle version]. Available from Amazon.com

Cook, F. C., & Fuller, J. M. (1966). *The Bible Commentary (Barnes Notes on the Old Testament): Proverbs–Ezekiel*. Grand Rapids, MI: Baker Book House.

Delitzsch, F. (2001). *Commentary on the Old Testament* (Vol. 6). (M. G. Easton, Trans.). Peabody, MA: Hendrickson Publishers. (Original work published 1866-1891).

Jamieson, R., Fausset, A. R., & Brown, D. (2011). *A Commentary, Critical and Explanatory, on the Old and New Testaments* [Kindle version]. Available from Amazon.com

Zerr, E. M. (1954). *Bible Commentary: Old Testament* (Vol. 2). Bowling Green, KY: Guardian of Truth Foundation.

Scripture Index

Genesis
1:1, 24
1:26-2:2, 24
1:27, 260
2:18-24, 189, 201
2:18, 183, 191, 192, 194, 197
2:24, 192
3:22-24, 31
4:1-2, 201
39:7-10, 184

Exodus
3:8, 95
20:12, 107, 208
20:15, 155
23:2-3, 154
23:3, 243

Leviticus
5:1, 215
19:18, 5

Deuteronomy
5:16, 12
27:16, 107
32:35, 222, 226, 263

1 Samuel
15:22, 40, 264

1 Kings
3:5-12, 1-2, 70
3:6, 4
3:7, 4
3:8, 4

3:9, 5
3:11, 4
10:6-7, 2-3
11:1-8, 5-6

2 Chronicles
16:9, 252

Job
9:3, 252
14:1, 159

Psalm
19:10, 28
34:15-16, 253, 264
36:1, 257
58:9, 54
119:160, 28
133:1, 108

Proverbs
1:1-6, i
1:1, 1
1:4, ii, 186
1:5, iii
1:6, iii
1:7, 9, 13, 56, 59, 254
1:8, 6, 11
1:9, 32
1:10-19, 219
1:10, 219, 221
1:11-12, 219
1:13-14, 215, 220
1:15-16, 220
1:17-19, 220
1:19, 215, 220

1:20-33, 13-14
1:20-21, 14, 19, 21
1:20, 7
1:22-23, 186
1:22, 15
1:23, 15
1:24-26, 53
1:24-25, 14, 16
1:26-27, 16
1:28-30, 16
1:31-32, 17
1:33, 18
2:1-5, 64
2:2, 34
2:6-10, 69
2:7, 34
2:10-22, 33-34
2:10-11, 34
2:12-15, 35
2:12, 35
2:16-19, 35
2:20, 35
2:21-22, 36
3:1-7, 61
3:1-4, 11, 14
3:1, 12, 62
3:2, 12
3:3, 12
3:4, 13
3:5-8, 37, 52, 261
3:5-7, 73
3:5-6, 62
3:6, 20
3:7, 20
3:8, 20
3:9-10, 138

3:11-12, 78
3:13-26, 30
3:13, 30
3:14-15, 30
3:16, 31
3:17, 31
3:18, 8, 31
3:19-20, 32
3:21, 32
3:22, 32
3:23, 32
3:24, 33
3:25-26, 33
3:27-28, 223
3:29, 224
3:30, 232
3:31-33, 229
3:33-35, 53
3:35, 74
4:1-2, 268
4:5, 4, 7, 268
4:7, 7
4:8-9, 32
4:10-13, 62-63
4:10, 63
4:13, 63
4:14-19, 221
4:14-15, 221
4:16, 221
4:17, 222
4:18-19, 222
4:20-27, 61-62
4:20-21, 268
4:20, 11, 62
4:23, 56, 63, 92, 153, 192
4:24, 114
4:25-27, 269
4:25, 62
4:26, 62
4:27, 62
5:1-14, 35, 173-174, 192
5:1-2, 174, 182

5:1, 175
5:3-4, 174
5:5, 175
5:6, 175
5:7-8, 175
5:9-11, 175-176
5:10, 178, 188
5:12-14, 176
5:15-20, 192
5:15, 192
5:16, 192
5:18, 192
5:19, 192
5:20, 192
5:21, 259
5:22-23, 37-38
6:1-5, 149-150
6:6-11, 131
6:8, 132
6:12-15, 38
6:15, 82
6:16-19, 91, 257
6:20-24, 182
6:20, 64, 177-178
6:23, 64, 80
6:24-35, 35, 80, 177, 192
6:24, 177
6:25, 178, 179
6:26, 176, 178, 182, 188
6:27-29, 178-179
6:30-31, 179
6:32, 179
6:33-35, 179, 184
7:1-27, 35, 180-181, 192
7:1-5, 181-182
7:6-7, 182
7:8-9, 182
7:10, 182, 183
7:11-12, 183
7:11, 186
7:13-21, 174
7:13-17, 183
7:13, 184

7:14, 184
7:15, 184
7:16-17, 184
7:17-18, 185
7:18, 184, 189
7:19-20, 184
7:21-23, 185
7:22-27, 80
7:22, 185
7:24-27, 185
7:26-27, 175
8:1-11, 18
8:1-3, 19
8:1, 11
8:2-3, 21
8:4-6, 11
8:4-5, 19
8:5-6, 186
8:6-8, 19
8:9, 20
8:10-11, 20, 29
8:12, 7, 242
8:13, 257
8:15-16, 242
8:17, 70
8:18-19, 7, 29
8:20, 153
8:21, 31
8:22-36, 22-23
8:22-31, 252
8:22-29, 32
8:22, 23, 27, 251
8:23, 24, 251
8:24-31, 251
8:24-25, 24
8:27-29, 24-25
8:30-31, 25
8:32-33, 25
8:32, 24
8:34-35, 26
8:36, 26
9:1-6, 21
9:1-3, 21

9:4-6, 21-22
9:4, 186, 188
9:7-8, 83, 84, 85
9:8, 85
9:9, 70
9:10, 13, 56, 59, 74
9:11, 31
9:12, 39
9:13-18, 35, 185-186, 192
9:13, 186
9:14-16, 186
9:15, 186
9:16-17, 187, 188
9:18, 187
10:1, 202
10:2, 135
10:4-5, 135
10:8, 66, 67, 71
10:9, 33
10:10, 116
10:11, 103
10:12, 231
10:13-14, 116
10:13, 43
10:14, 71
10:15, 139, 146
10:16, 53
10:17, 63
10:19, 117, 119
10:20, 104
10:21, 109
10:22, 144
10:23, 7, 87
10:24, 47
10:25, 54
10:27-30, 54
10:31-32, 104
11:1, 155
11:2, 73
11:3-8, 47-48, 203
11:3, 48
11:4, 48, 145

11:5, 48
11:6, 48
11:7, 48
11:8, 48
11:9, 110
11:10-11, 226
11:12-13, 116-117
11:14, 64, 73
11:15, 150
11:16, 136, 190
11:17-19, 48
11:20-21, 55, 203
11:20, 266
11:22, 190
11:23, 92-93
11:24-26, 140
11:27, 50
11:28, 145
11:29, 41
11:30, 32, 40
12:1, 80
12:2, 53
12:4, 189
12:5, 93, 153
12:7, 55
12:8, 49, 55
12:9, 147
12:10, 92, 142
12:11, 136
12:13, 106, 112
12:14, 31
12:15, 65
12:16, 95
12:17-19, 113
12:17, 113
12:18, 94, 113
12:19, 113
12:21, 50
12:22, 92, 114
12:23, 116
12:24, 126, 146
12:25, 109
12:26, 224

12:27, 129
12:28, 32
13:1, 78
13:3, 118
13:4, 128, 146
13:5, 92
13:7, 139
13:9, 49
13:10, 65
13:11, 135
13:12, 159
13:13-15, 50
13:15, 37, 41, 55
13:16, 87
13:17, 50
13:18, 80
13:20, 60, 65, 218
13:21, 50
13:22, 140, 209
13:23, 157
13:24, 43, 205
13:25, 51
14:1, 191
14:2, 256
14:3, 43, 106
14:4, 142
14:5, 114, 156
14:6, 71
14:7, 213, 214
14:8, 72
14:9, 55
14:10, 159
14:11, 55
14:12, 36, 65, 76, 104, 261
14:13, 160, 162
14:14, 51
14:15, 65, 66
14:16-17, 93
14:18, 70
14:19, 41
14:20, 148
14:21, 233

14:22, 56
14:23, 123, 125
14:24, 145
14:25, 115
14:26-27, 257
14:26, 56
14:28, 245
14:29-30, 94
14:31, 234
14:32, 8, 54
14:33, 71
14:34, 237
15:3, 252, 259
15:5, 80
15:6, 51
15:7, 119
15:8-9, 264, 265
15:8, 266
15:10, 81, 82
15:11, 259
15:12, 65, 83
15:13, 160, 161
15:14, 68, 71
15:15, 160
15:16, 258
15:17, 201
15:18, 231
15:19, 126
15:20, 202
15:21, 93
15:22, 64, 73
15:23, 109
15:24, 31
15:26, 105, 265
15:27, 136
15:29, 253
15:32, 79
15:33, 74
16:1-7, 254-255
16:1, 169, 255
16:2, 255
16:3, 169, 255
16:4-5, 255

16:6, 256
16:7, 256, 258
16:8, 147
16:9, 169
16:10-12, 243
16:11, 157
16:13, 244
16:14-15, 238, 249
16:16, 29
16:17, 93
16:18-19, 75
16:20, 66
16:22, 83
16:25, 36, 65, 76, 104, 261
16:26, 124
16:27-28, 110-111
16:29, 229
16:31, 60
16:32, 95
16:33, 262
17:1, 201
17:2, 207
17:3, 260, 261
17:4, 121
17:5, 225, 234
17:6, 209
17:7, 103, 244
17:9, 117
17:10, 83
17:11, 43
17:12, 213
17:13-14, 232
17:15, 266
17:16, 59
17:17, 211
17:19, 227, 228
17:21, 202, 203
17:22, 161
17:23, 154, 156
17:24, 66
17:25, 202
17:26, 245, 247

17:27-28, 117
17:27, 95
17:28, 117
18:2, 66, 67, 71, 119
18:3, 39
18:5, 154
18:9, 127
18:10-11, 139, 146
18:10, 262, 263
18:12, 75
18:13, 118
18:14, 161
18:15, 68, 71
18:16, 148
18:17-18, 156
18:17, 118
18:19, 229
18:21, 108
18:22, 189
18:24, 217, 218
19:1, 93
19:2-3, 39
19:4, 148, 217
19:5, 93, 158
19:6-7, 148, 217
19:9, 113
19:11, 92
19:12, 238
19:13, 202
19:14, 189
19:15, 127, 130
19:16, 54
19:17, 233, 234
19:18, 205, 206
19:19, 43
19:20, 63, 80
19:21, 252
19:22, 92
19:23, 257
19:24, 129
19:25, 84
19:26, 208
19:27, 81

19:28, 156, 158
19:29, 42
20:1, 163, 222
20:2, 247
20:3, 228
20:4, 127, 131, 141
20:5, 88
20:6, 96, 98
20:7, 203
20:8, 238, 240, 245
20:9, 91
20:10, 155
20:11, 98
20:12, 253
20:13, 131
20:14, 137, 138
20:15, 104
20:16, 150
20:17, 106
20:18, 64
20:19, 107, 216
20:20, 107
20:21, 137
20:22, 263
20:23, 155
20:25, 118
20:26, 239, 240 245, 247
20:27, 259
20:28, 240
20:29, 60, 124
20:30, 80
21:2, 260
21:3, 263, 264, 266
21:4, 91
21:5, 125, 127, 137
21:6, 136, 137
21:7, 157, 229
21:8, 93
21:9, 191, 192
21:10, 228
21:11, 84
21:12, 68
21:13, 234

21:14, 149
21:15, 153
21:16, 41
21:19, 192
21:21, 31
21:22, 33
21:23, 113-114
21:24, 91
21:25-26, 128
21:27, 39
21:30, 251
21:31, 170
22:1, 99
22:2, 260
22:4, 31
22:5, 50
22:6, 8, 204
22:7, 150
22:8, 41
22:9, 233, 234
22:10, 216
22:11, 247
22:12, 252
22:13, 130, 132
22:14, 174
22:15, 43, 202, 204, 206
22:16, 234
22:17, 60
22:20-21, 60
22:22-23, 234
22:24-25, 214
22:26-27, 150
22:28, 154
22:29, 125
23:1-3, 248
23:4-5, 101, 146
23:6-8, 216
23:7, 56, 106
23:9, 67, 213
23:10-11, 154
23:12, 60, 78
23:13-14, 43, 206
23:15-16, 202, 203

23:15, 203
23:16, 203
23:17, 258
23:18, 171
23:19, 63
23:20-21, 163-164, 168
23:22, 63
23:23, 27
23:24-25, 203
23:26, 63
23:27-28, 187
23:29-35, 164-165, 168
23:29-30, 165
23:31-32, 165
23:33, 166
23:34-35, 166
23:35, 166
24:1-2, 213
24:3-4, 31
24:5, 33
24:6, 64, 73
24:8-9, 39, 55
24:9, 39
24:11, 225
24:12, 114, 213, 256, 261
24:13-14, 268
24:16, 51
24:17-18, 225
24:19-20, 40, 42
24:20, 108
24:21-22, 214
24:21, 246, 254
24:23, 154
24:24-26, 120
24:25, 120
24:27, 141
24:28, 232
24:29, 225
24:30-34, 127-128
24:33-34, 131
25:1, 1
25:2-3, 240
25:5, 241, 244

25:6-7, 248
25:8-10, 228
25:11, 105, 109
25:14, 115
25:15, 109
25:16, 95, 99
25:17, 230
25:19, 97
25:20, 162
25:21-22, 226
25:24, 192
25:25, 105
25:27, 95
25:28, 96
26:1, 44
26:3, 43, 82
26:4-5, 120
26:6, 97
26:7, 72
26:8, 44
26:9, 72
26:11, 88
26:12, 76
26:13, 130, 132
26:14, 129, 130
26:15, 129, 130
26:16, 76, 130
26:17, 230
26:18-19, 230
26:20-28, 111-112
26:20-21, 112
26:20, 216
26:22, 112
26:23-26, 112
26:27, 112
27:1-2, 111
27:1, 170
27:2, 91
27:3-4, 94
27:3, 111
27:5, 85
27:6, 211
27:7, 99
27:8, 100
27:9, 212
27:10, 227
27:11, 203, 208
27:13, 150
27:14, 218
27:15-16, 191
27:17, 212
27:19, 92
27:20, 100, 101
27:21, 98
27:22, 84
27:23-27, 143, 240
27:24, 241
28:1, 57
28:2, 237-238
28:3, 235
28:4, 245
28:5, 153, 156
28:6, 93
28:7, 215
28:8, 138
28:9, 264, 265, 266
28:10, 121
28:11, 76-77
28:12, 240
28:13, 74
28:14, 67
28:15-16, 246
28:17, 40
28:19, 8, 127, 146
28:20, 125, 137
28:21, 154
28:22, 137
28:23, 85
28:24, 208
28:25-26, 52
28:28, 239
29:1, 82
29:2, 239, 240
29:3, 176, 178, 188
29:4, 242, 243
29:5, 224
29:7, 154
29:8, 94
29:10, 92
29:11, 95
29:12, 244
29:13, 158
29:14, 242, 243
29:15, 43, 206
29:16, 42
29:17, 206
29:18, 36
29:19, 79
29:20, 119
29:21, 227
29:22, 94
29:23, 75
29:24, 215
29:25, 263
29:26, 248
30:1, 1, 75, 108
30:2-5, 74
30:5-6, 252
30:7-8, 114
30:8-9, 143-144
30:10, 232
30:11, 208
30:12-13, 77
30:15-16, 100
30:17, 208
30:20, 188
30:21, 125
30:22, 125
30:24-28, 132
30:25, 132
30:26, 132
30:27, 132
30:28, 132
30:29-31, 239
30:32-33, 108
31:1, 1
31:4-7, 167
31:4-5, 167
31:4, 168

31:5, 163, 167, 168, 222
31:6-7, 165, 168
31:7, 168
31:8-9, 243
31:10-31, 193-194
31:10, 194, 198
31:11-12, 194
31:11, 196
31:13, 195, 196, 197
31:14, 195
31:15, 195
31:16, 196
31:17, 196
31:18, 196
31:19, 196, 197
31:20, 196
31:21-22, 197
31:23, 197
31:24, 195, 196, 197
31:25, 197
31:26, 198
31:27, 198
31:28-29, 198
31:30, 190, 198
31:31, 199

Ecclesiastes
1:17-18, 69
2:12-17, 69
9:10, 123, 146
9:11, 262
12:7, 260
12:13, 254

Isaiah
5:20, 120
29:6, 54
31:1, 170
66:15, 54

Jeremiah
10:23, 76, 261
16:17, 252

Lamentations
3:27, 124

Ezekiel
18:32, 17

Hosea
8:7, 41, 54

Nahum
1:3, 54

Zechariah
12:1, 260

Matthew
5:28, 178
6:14-15, 234
6:33, 51
7:12, 49, 225-226
7:13-14, 37
16:26, 42
22:39, 5

Luke
10:7, 141
14:7-11, 248

John
8:44, 114
14:15, 256
17:17, 28

Acts
1:23-26, 262
8:22, 263
10:35, 254
17:26, 201, 260
24:26-27, 149

Romans
1:5, 53
3:18, 257

3:23, 91
6:16, 38
6:17-22, 53
6:23, 38, 41, 53
12:19-20, 226
12:19, 263
13:4, 239
16:26, 53

1 Corinthians
1:20-21, 19
2:11, 160, 259-260
3:19, 19, 72
5:9-10, 164

2 Corinthians
5:1, 171
5:10, 260, 261
8:12, 223

Galatians
6:7, 41

Ephesians
4:14, 65
4:28, 128

Philippians
4:8, 56

Colossians
3:2, 171

1 Thessalonians
4:11, 247-248

1 Timothy
2:11, 183
4:2, 38, 82
5:20, 121
5:23, 168
6:3-5, 51
6:18-19, 233-234

2 Timothy
3:13, 42
4:3, 121

Titus
1:2, 114
2:4-5, 183
2:12, 38

Hebrews
2:1, 26
4:12-13, 259
4:12, 42
4:13, 252, 259
9:27, 260
11:25, 40, 185
12:5-10, 78
12:11, 78, 79, 207
13:4, 192

James
1:5-6, 3
1:5, 69-70
1:17, 4, 233
1:19-20, 39
1:19, 118
1:21, 4
3:1, 121
3:5-6, 111
3:8, 117
4:13-16, 170
5:13, 162

1 Peter
1:3-4, 171
2:14, 245
3:5-6, 191
3:12, 253, 264
5:5-6, 75

2 Peter
3:9, 17

1 John
1:8, 91
1:9, 263
2:1, 264
3:4, 265

3 John
1:4, 203

Revelation
22:2, 32

Additional Resources

If you are interested in using this material for either a personal or group Bible study, you can download a free PDF file with questions for each chapter at the following web address:

www.gospelarmory.com/resources

The link above will also have similar study guides for other books that have been published by Gospel Armory:

Vanity of Vanities: Notes on Ecclesiastes

The Root of the Problem: Why We Sin & How We Can Overcome

These study guides are also available for free in PDF format.

www.ingramcontent.com/pod-product-compliance
Lightning Source LLC
LaVergne TN
LVHW041610070426
835507LV00008B/180